M000200665

The Magick of M

Often students of metaphysics have difficulty achieving results strictly through visualization and meditation. They become discouraged if they don't get results. Others find it difficult to concentrate; they still have on their minds that last phone call, argument with the boss, or troubles with the kids. These kinds of mundane energies can block our higher perceptions.

Now you can learn to move from the outer world, with its hassles and distractions, to the inner realms of intuition and creativity through the physical movement, postures, and gestures of *Magickal Dance*.

Dance is a dynamic tool for awakening and stirring up the subtle forces and energies of life. It is an outer expression of an inner spirit.

Dance and movement are natural to the universe. Plants will move gracefully to face the sun and wave in a breeze. Birds and animals display magnificent arrays of plumage and posture for everything from courtship to aggression. Dance is natural and vital to humans as well.

We are all musical and have rhythm. It is intrinsic to our nature. We have been surrounded by music since the moment of conception—from the sounds carried to us through the amniotic fluids during pregnancy, to the rhythmic beat of our own hearts. Who has not seen a mother sing and hum while softly rocking a crying child into calmness?

The human body is designed for movement. True magickal movement and dance can be performed by anyone. No formal training is required to utilize the powerful effects of sacred dance. It enables us to transcend our usual consciousness and perceptions. It enables us to reach another level of being.

This book reveals simple methods of dancing new energy into your life. You will discover that the energies invoked through magickal movement function less through your talent than through your participation! If you can move any part of your body, you can participate in magickal dance—even if it is only through the flickering of an eye or the rhythm of breath!

Magickal dance is a celebration of life. It reawakens the child within us that responds to the primal rhythmic forces of the universe. Through dance, we invoke, challenge and direct these forces to manifest the abundance, prosperity, fulfillment, and joy we desire. Through magickal movement, we can all learn to become the priests and priestesses of our own lives.

ABOUT THE AUTHOR

Ted Andrews is a full-time author, student, and teacher in the metaphysical and spiritual fields. He conducts seminars, symposiums, workshops, and lectures throughout the country on many facets of ancient mysticism, focusing on translating esoteric material to make it comprehensible and practical for everyone. This includes taking ancient scriptures, literatures, and teachings and resynthesizing them for use by the modern spiritual student.

Ted is certified in basic hypnosis and acupressure, and is involved in the study and use of herbs as an alternative path in heath care. Ted is active in the holistic healing field, focusing strongly on esoteric forms of healing with sound, music, and voice. Trained in piano, he also employs the Celtic harp, bamboo flute, shaman rattles, Tibetan bells, the Tibetan Singing Bowl, and quartz crystal bowls to create individual healing therapies and induce higher states of consciousness.

Ted is a clairvoyant and works with past life analysis and synthesis, aura interpretation, dreams, numerology, and the tarot. He utilizes and teaches ancient techniques to accelerate and develop an individual's latent potential.

He is a contributing author to various metaphysical magazines with published articles on various topics including, *Occult Christianity*, *Working With Our Angelic Brethren*, and the *Metaphysical Mirrors Within Our Lives*.

TO WRITE TO THE AUTHOR

If you wish to contact the author or would like more information about this book, please write to the author in care of Llewellyn Worldwide and we will forward your request. Both the author and publisher appreciate hearing from you and learning of your enjoyment of his book and how it has helped you. Llewellyn Worldwide cannot guarantee that every letter written to the author can be answered, but all will be forwarded. Please write to:

Ted Andrews
c/o Llewellyn Worldwide
P.O. Box 64383-004, St. Paul, MN 55164 - 0383, U.S.A.

Please enclose a self-addressed, stamped envelope for reply, or $1.00 to cover costs.
If outside U.S.A., enclose international postal reply coupon.

FREE CATALOG FROM LLEWELLYN WORLDWIDE

For more than 90 years Llewellyn has brought its readers knowledge in the fields of metaphysics and human potential. Learn about the newest books in spiritual guidance, natural healing, astrology, occult philosophy and more. Enjoy book reviews, new age articles, a calendar of events, plus current advertised products and services. To get your free copy of *The Llewellyn New Worlds*, send you name and address to:

The Llewellyn New Worlds
P.O. Box 64383-004, St. Paul, MN 55164-0383, U.S.A.

Llewellyn's Practical Guide to Personal Power Series

MAGICKAL DANCE

Your Body as an Instrument of Power

TED ANDREWS

1993
Llewellyn Publications
St. Paul, Minnesota 55164-0383

Magickal Dance. Copyright © 1993 by Ted Andrews. All rights reserved. Printed in the United States of America. No part of this book may be used or reproduced in any manner whatsoever without written permission from Llewellyn Publications except in the case of brief quotations embodied in critical articles and reviews.

First Edition
First Printing

Cover design by Chris Wells
Illustrations by Hrana Janto

Library of Congress Cataloging-in-publication Data
Andrews, Ted. 1952-
    Magickal dance: your body as an instrument of power/Ted Andrews.
        p. cm. — (Llewellyn's practical guides to personal power)
    Includes bibliographical references.
    ISBN 0-87542-004-4
    1. Magic 2. Dancing—Miscellanea.   I. Title. II. Series: Llewellyn
practical guides to personal power.
BF 1623.D35A53 1992
133.4'3—dc20   92-18981
                                                                    CIP

Llewellyn Publications
A Division of Llewellyn Worldwide, Ltd.
P.O. Box 64383, St. Paul, MN 55164-0383

About the Llewellyn's Practical Guides to Personal Power

To some people, the idea that "magick" is *practical* comes as a surprise. It shouldn't!

The entire basis for magick is to exercise influence over one's personal world in order to satisfy our needs and goals. And, while this magick is also concerned with psychological transformation and spiritual growth, even the spiritual life must be built on firm material foundations.

Here are practical and usable techniques that will help you to a better life, will help you attain things you want, will help you in your personal growth and development. *Moreover, these books can change your life, dynamically, positively!*

The material world and the psychic are intertwined, and it is this that establishes the magickal link: that mind-soul-spirit can as easily influence the material as vice versa.

Psychic powers and magickal practices can, and should, be used in one's daily life. Each of us has many wonderful, but yet underdeveloped talents and powers—surely we have an evolutionary obligation to make full use of our human potentials! Mind and body work together, and magick is simply the extension of this interaction into dimensions beyond the limits normally conceived. *Why be limited?*

All things you will ever want or be must have their start in your mind. In these books you are given practical guidance to develop your inner powers and apply them to your everyday needs. These abilities will eventually belong to everybody through natural evolution, but you can learn and develop them now!

This series of books will help you achieve such things as success, happiness, miracles, powers of ESP, healing, out-of-body travel, clairvoyance, divination, extended powers of mind and body, communication with non-physical beings, and knowledge by non-material means!

We've always known of things like this—seemingly supernormal achievements, often performed by quite ordinary people. We are told that we normally use only ten percent of our human potential. We are taught that faith can move mountains, that love heals all hurt, that miracles do occur. We believe these things to be true, but most people lack practical knowledge of them.

The books in this series form a full library of magickal knowledge and practice.

Other Books by Ted Andrews

Simplified Magick
Imagick
The Sacred Power in Your Name
How to See and Read the Aura
How to Uncover Your Past Lives
Dream Alchemy: Shaping Our Dream to Transform Our Lives
The Magical Name
Sacred Sounds: Transformation Through Music and Word
How to Meet and Work with Spirit Guides
How to Heal with Color

Forthcoming Books by Ted Andrews

The Healer's Manual
Enchantment of the Faerie Realm
The Occult Christ
Animal Speak

Dedication

To the Holy Child within
who can help us rediscover the magick and joy
of song and dance!

TABLE OF CONTENTS

Part One

The Basics of Ritual Dance

CHAPTER ONE

THE MAGICKAL POWER
IN DANCE

Dance is one of the most powerful forms of magickal ritual. It is a dynamic tool for awakening and stirring the subtle forces and energies of life. True sacred dance is a means of focusing and directing consciousness through physical behavior. It is an outer expression of the inner spirit.

Magickal dance can be performed by anyone. No formal training is required to utilize the powerful effects of sacred dance. Dances for higher states of consciousness are simple, individual, and passionate. They do not require great space, for when a dance pattern is created for specific effects, it will also create an illusion of great space, power, and time. It is simply a matter of imbuing movement with greater significance and focus. It is not the talent that invokes the energy but rather the participation.

Dance and movement is natural to the universe. Plants will move in graceful and rhythmic ways. They turn to face the sun; they wave in a breeze; they grow in spirals and other exquisite forms. Birds have their own movements and dance, spreading their wings and plumage in magnificent displays of courtship or strength. All animals have unique dances as well to show strength, aggression, or just high-spirited fun.

3

The human body is designed for movement. Movement is as natural and as important to life as breathing. Like breathing, it fills us with energy. It enables us to transcend our usual perceptions and consciousness. Movement balances, heals, awakens, and energizes. It generates psychic energy for strength, for enlightenment, for life, and even for death.

The purpose of all physical, ritual behavior is to direct and focus the consciousness. Humans have a unique ability to block their own growth process. Directed physical behavior, such as dance, can help us overcome this tendency. It aligns our physical responses and energies with our spiritual goals and helps us maintain contact with the higher forces of life.

Dance links the hemispheres of the brain, joining the intuitive and the rational. Every movement and gesture creates electrical changes in the body and the mind. Through magickal dance, the movements and their essence are experienced on subtler levels.

The central nervous system and the neuro-muscular systems transform musical rhythms into a movement pattern. We can become driven by it and led away from our traditional perceptions of the world. In the past, individuals would surrender to these rhythms and be possessed by them. Examples of this can be found within the Voudon religions of the Caribbean. Today we must learn to ride the rhythms in full consciousness of those inner worlds.

All dance is gesture, and we each have gestures that are uniquely our own. They give us color and individuality. Gesture links the outer person with the inner and serves to bridge us to our more divine aspects. For gesture and movement to become empowered, they must be consciously directed and infused with significance.

In the modern world, the magickal power in dance has been diminished. Actual energies are created and awakened in all forms of dance, even in modern social settings. In these, magnetic energies are stimulated, but the result is a touching of the romantic rather than the sacred realms. Many of the ancient societies stressed continual watchfulness and control over dance energies. They recognized a therapeutic and an educational value to dance, but they focused upon its sacred aspect. They knew that the male and female participants were not just dancers; rather, by dancing, they became priests and priestesses.

Magickal dance is a means of transcending our humanity. Through it you can gain control over normally automatic responses by evoking lower emotions and energies and then channeling them through the dance. Magickal dance is an art that fires our vitality, revives depleted energies, and awakens individual creativity and improvisational abilities.

All human activity is a dance ritual, but we still must learn new approaches to it. Non-believers and non-participants will never understand the true ritual power of dance. For these individuals, the magickal dance will be little more than a window display. The dervishes will only be entertainers. The Catholic mass becomes little more than a spectacle. We must remember that religious ritual of any kind is not, and should never be, performed for its own sake. This may be the primary problem with the weekly mass!

Ritual—especially magickal dance ritual—should be performed as a way of reaching another level of consciousness or being. It should be a way of releasing spiritual meaning into our lives. Dance ritual is not meant to be performed for audiences, which profanes it in many ways. We must participate in and become the priests and priestesses of the dance ritual.

Our participation in magickal dance requires us to remember that energies are not created by the dance but simply invoked and challenged by it. We must remember that the energies function less through our talent for dancing than through our participation! Thus, anyone who can move any part of his or her body can participate in magickal dance, even if only through the flickering of eyes or the rhythm of breath.

Magickal Dance Yesterday and Today

In our recent history, we find religious dancing taking place within churches and temples. Earlier groups created dance temples by marking off sacred circles for the dance on the Earth itself. One common theme was the imitation of angels dancing in heavenly rings around the throne of God. This led to many of the circle dances which will be discussed later in the book.

Sacred and magickal dancing has been a functioning part of every society and civilization throughout the world. The shamans and priests/priestesses used music and dance to induce trance states. In all of the dances, intense feelings and bodily movements were related. In many cases, such as in the ancient Kachina rites, the participants became reflections of different powers in the universe.

A basic premise behind esoteric teachings around the world is that we all are a microcosm—a reflection or miniature of the macrocosm or universe. We have all the energies of the universe within us. Sacred dance was a means of stimulating them and bringing them into expression out to the deeper levels of our consciousness.

The Kachina dancers used round or circle dances to imitate the path of the sun. Chain dances were used to link male and female energies, to stimulate fertility, and to bind heaven and earth. There were thread-and-rope dances, as with the threads of Ariadne, threads that lead the dancer to the secret knowledge within the maze of life.

The power of movement and dance was even infused into the martial arts, especially in the Eastern world. A kata is a series of movements in the martial arts. While some interpret it as a combat discipline, it can also be seen as a martial arts dance. A kata can be translated as "how one behaves" or a "moving book." The practitioner, in more ancient times, would record what he learned in a sequence of moves. The outer form expressed an inward movement or purpose.

In Kung Fu the forms and movements are based upon animals—praying mantis, hawk, eagle, a tiger, etc. This facilitated the study of nature and helped attune the student to animal aspects of nature. The mimicking and imitating of animals will be explored more fully later in the book.

In the Ninja tradition, postures and hand poses have great significance. The Ninja could generate power based on the mystical idea of redirecting the intrinsic energy of nature through their hands. Each hand and finger symbolizes an intrinsic force and attribute of the body.

In India, the sacred dancing girls, or devadasis, were married to the gods. Their dances represented the life of the god to whom they were married.

Ancient Egypt was also a great dancing center. The importance of dance to the ancient Egyptians is illustrated in the hieroglyphs, where dancers are extensively depicted. The Egyptian love for dance was widely felt throughout the ancient world. The Cadiz, the sacred dancing school in Spain, was another great center of ancient dancing and was Egyptian in character.

The Greek and the Roman mystery schools were strong in dance ritual. Dance, along with music, formed an essential part of the magickal and healing arts in the Orphic, Eleusinian, and Bacchic mysteries. The snakelike winding of the Greek farandole dance of Provence symbolized the journey to the middle of the labyrinth—the pattern of the passage of the dead to the land of the afterlife. This journey was a common theme in many areas of the world.

Sacred dance revolves around themes and patterns that stimulate multiple responses. A dance for higher states of consciousness is simple, personal, and passionate—fusing the mind and body. The degree to which energy is invoked is determined by the participation and the significance associated with the movement. Every gesture and movement must be symbolic. The more meaning we attach to movement, the greater the release of power.

Sacred dance helps us to transcend our humanity. The transcendental aspect of dance has been neglected for centuries, yet each of us has the ability to re-awaken it. Magickal dance is more than just a symbolic expression of an individual's personal beliefs. At the root of most ceremonial use of dance is sympathetic magick. The movements and gestures create thoughtforms, vortices of energy. The fusion of thought and action manifests a particular pattern of energy in the physical realm.

Throughout the rest of this book, you will learn to choreograph your own evolution. You will awaken your own creative energies through dance. The exercises and dynamics in this book are only a foundation. They are merely starting points. Do not allow the movements to become rote and always allow for individual expression and variation. As you do, you will find yourself dancing the Tree of Life, which joins heaven and earth within you.

Magickal Postures and Positions

Some physical movements and postures stimulate different levels of consciousness. And there are some which activate celestial energies, drawing them more emphatically into play within the physical realm. We can learn to use these movements and postures to create a mind-set that enables easier access to these energies.

Frequently, the student of the metaphysical and psychic world will have difficulty achieving tangible results through mere meditation. Often individuals will sit to meditate, but they may still be thinking of that last phone call, the argument with the boss, or troubles with the kids. These kinds of mundane energies can block our higher perceptive abilities. Physical movements enable a person to move from outer world consciousness, with all of its hassles and distractions, to the inner world more fluidly.

Working with the physical movements will deliver results more quickly and effectively than passive meditation. Movement creates electrical changes in the body and mind, which facilitate the accessing of subtle energies. Physical activity causes the mind to shift gears. It has to concentrate on the movements and gestures. The postures, positions, movements, and gestures throughout this book will help you make transitions from the outer to the inner world, and back again, more easily and effectively.

Gestures, postures, and movements express the inexpressible. They utilize both aspects of the brain, especially when we imbue them with significance. The more meaning we ascribe to them, the more empowered they become. They are direct, potent ways of communicating with the divine forces operating around us and within us. They aid us in concentration, so we can manifest our highest capacities.

The Eastern world has recognized the spiritual value of movement for ages. Fortunately, there is a growing integration of Eastern and Western philosophies and techniques. We can apply some Eastern methods of movement specifically to Western forms of magick and mysticism. The Eastern yoga movements and postures are simply outer expressions, stimulating and representing inner degrees of consciousness.

Yoga asanas are designed to be meditations themselves, leading to greater depths of energy. Applying them to Western mystical and magickal traditions reinforces the idea that there truly is nothing new under the sun. There are simply different variations. All gods are aspects of the same god, and we each have the responsibility of finding the methods or combination of methods which will most effectively awaken the divine within ourselves.

In yoga, kriya is a movement, asana, mudra, or exercise to produce an altered state of consciousness. There is an outer kriya which involves asanas and mudras (postures and gestures)—basic physical expressions, as well an inner aspect. When we learn to dance magickally, we are using an outer form to express an inner energy. We learn to apply physical expressions to inner realities. These physical movements awaken and draw out our inner spiritual energies. Different movements will activate different energies—whether they be intuitive, creative, protective, or healing.

Postures are a way of physically communicating with the divine within us. As we will see in chapter five, many postures and movements arose from a ritual mimicking of animals and nature to establish a magickal contact with its forces.

Different postures and movements will activate different energies and forces. Learning to combine, control, and direct the forces and energies through dance is an individually creative process. Movement is basic to our body's shape and function. Dance allows the body to worship. Magickal dance releases tremendous power. It intoxicates you and helps you become more aware of where your body is in a given space and time. Movement will stimulate a tangible awareness that the body houses the divine spirit. To make the most of these exercises, keep in mind the following:

1. Allow for individual expression and variation while performing the exercises.

2. Do not allow the exercises to become rote. Imbue your magickal dance with greater significance and power each time you use it.

3. Keep your movements simple and fluid.

4. Magickal dance movements are tremendously empowering to meditations when performed before and after the meditation.

5. The more we work with the movements, the easier they become, and the more energy is released to us.

Magickal Dance Exercise:
The Dancer's Pose

Movements and postures for balance are beneficial before and after any ritual or meditation. They stabilize the energies that are activated through the movement so we can experience them more effectively. This will be explored more fully in the next chapter, but this is a good introductory exercise for this aspect.

The pose of the dancer is shown on the opposite page. This is what we are becoming when we work with the magickal aspects of movement. We are becoming the great Dancer of Life. We are learning to choreograph our life and our inner resources for greater expression. The dancer's pose is an effective way to begin any dance ritual or meditation because it balances the hemispheres of the brain and creates a shift in focus and consciousness. It can also be effectively used before and after rituals or meditations that don't involve dance.

Begin the pose by standing, facing straight ahead. Choose one leg to balance yourself upon. Raise the foot of the other leg behind you, and hold it with your hand. Raise the other hand up, pointing it forward and up. Keep your eyes straight ahead; it will help balance you. Now lean forward, and raise the leg you are holding up as high as is comfortable for you. See yourself as a dancer, making great leaps of consciousness, dancing from one realm to the next.

Now relax and stand straight again, with both feet flat on the ground. Now reverse legs, balancing in this pose on the opposite leg. You may find it easier to balance on one leg than the other, this can indicate you need to work at keeping harmony in your life. As you develop a greater ability to hold this pose, you develop a greater ability to maintain harmony in your life.

One of the most powerful ways of using this posture is in the creation of a magickal body. The magickal body is the ideal you—the new, more conscious you that is created through the dance. The magickal body is the you that is capable of manifesting and appearing in the manner most effective and powerful for your life. It is the ability to assume the manners and powers necessary for the life tasks you encounter.

The Dancer's Pose

The dancer's pose, by shifting our consciousness, helps to create and maintain balance in our life as we open up to those inner energies and more ethereal realms of life.

What is the highest, brightest, most creative image of yourself that you can imagine? What characteristics would you have? What abilities and energies would you be able to express? How would you ideally like others to see you? How would being that ideal you change your life at home and at work? If you could manifest those abilities now, how could you use them so no one would ever know?

Imagine it, envision it, know it can be real. If you can imagine it, it can be! When you change your imaginings, you change your world.

Now, as you assume this posture, see yourself becoming the ideal you with whatever form, image, and power you have imagined. Feel and see yourself shapeshifting into the ideal, magickal you that can work effectively in both the physical and spiritual world.

Within the magickal dance, everything is possible. It creates an intersection between the physical and the spiritual, the inner and the outer. It is a point of power that encompasses you. It becomes a space where you can learn to be capable of anything—where the magic of manifestation begins.

Visualize this ideal, magickal you, as if you are already it. See yourself, calling the ideal you forward through this position. Use this visualization with the movements at the beginning and the end of your rituals and meditations to give them greater power. Our magickal essence is a reflection of our higher, truer self. The movements and the imaging enable us to bring this essence into greater expression.

The Dancer Celebrates Life!

The Dancer Invokes Energy and Magic!

CHAPTER TWO

PREPARING FOR THE DANCE

Dance actualizes energy. Magickal dance is the art of ritual and creative movement which has the power to use the actualized energy to unite body and spirit. Anyone participating in magickal dance or ritual movement must begin to recognize the body as a medium for invoking and expressing energy, keeping in mind what he or she wishes to express with the body. Keeping this in mind, ritual movement must be approached in a manner that will facilitate the union of body and spirit.

As with any kind of movement or exercise, a warm-up is essential. Muscles must be prepared to move freely and maintain balance without risk of injury—even when the movements are to be simple and few. Some muscles can be strained in the magickal dance process if they are not stretched and accustomed to a broad reach. When the body is warmed up, the inner energy released through the ritual movement can become quite profound and extreme. Warming up develops the range of motion and balance, along with the magickal expression.

A good warm-up is gentle and relaxing. It should also be performed slowly. A proper, slow warm-up prepares the muscles, ligaments, and joints for more vigorous activity. The length of your warm-up will vary. A good rule of thumb is to warm-up to the point you are relaxed and loose. Warm-up exercises are important to do

15

before any dance routine, but are even more effective when performed every day to keep strong flexibility in your muscles.

If you already have an exercise program, you may wish to use your warm-up, or you may wish to use the warm-up described in this chapter. In either case, make sure that it works all major muscle groups.

Warm-up Exercises

1. Begin with some marching in place. This increases circulation overall in the body. Do this for several minutes.

2. Now we will loosen each area of the body in turn. As you stretch and loosen each area of the body throughout the rest of the warm-up, focus intently on the specific area. Visualize each area getting stronger and more flexible as you perform the exercises.

   Begin with the arms and shoulders. Swing the arms forward and back and around over the head. Keep the movements easy and smooth.

   Next, focus on the waist. Swing slowly from side to side. Do not allow your movements to become abrupt.

   Now loosen the hips. Alternate lifting each knee up. As you do, lift your arms at the same time. You may wish to tilt your pelvis forward slightly to take pressure off of the lower back.

   Now bend slightly and place your hands just above your knees. Begin to rotate your knees slowly, using a circular motion. Keep the movements small and slow.

   Sit on the floor. Lift one foot up. You may wish to hold your leg up with the aid of your hands. Slowly circle the ankle and foot in all directions. Point the toes, and pull them back. Loosen up this important joint, and then do the same with the other foot.

Leg Stretch Exercise

3. Once we have performed a general warm-up and loosening of the major muscles, we may wish to do a more concentrated stretching and loosening of muscles most likely to be used in the dance. The following is an excellent exercise to stretch the leg muscles and loosen them even further. Refer to photograph on the opposite page.

   Sit on the floor. Extend one leg outward. Try to keep the back of the knee flat against the floor, but do not worry if you cannot initially do so. It will come with time. Extend your leg to the degree comfortable for you. Draw the heel of one foot up into or near the crotch area of the body. The sole of the foot should rest against the inner thigh of the outstretched leg.

   Now slowly and gently extend your arms up over your head. Then slowly reach out with your arms to take hold of the calf of the extended leg. Holding the calf, pull your trunk down as far as possible without strain. Your head should be lowered. Hold for a count of ten. Slowly straighten up and then repeat at least three times or until the muscles feel warm and loose. Then switch legs.

4. This exercise, sometimes called the Butterfly, will promote flexibility in the knees. It will also stretch and strengthen the thigh muscles.

   Take a seated position with your head up and back straight. The soles of the feet should be placed together. Hold them with your hands, drawing the heels in as closely together as possible.

   Now pulling up slightly on the feet, lower your knees as near to the floor as possible without strain. Hold for a count of ten and release. Repeat three times.

   Initially, you may find that you can only lower the knees a few inches. This is fine. Hold your knees at whatever position you are able. As you stretch and work with this position, the stiff ligaments and muscles will gradually loosen.

The Butterfly

5.   The dancer's exercise, called urvasana in yoga, will firm and strengthen the legs, while helping develop balance and poise.

Perform this movement slowly. Don't worry if you lose your balance performing it. Repeat it at least three times, and practice it daily. Balance will be greatly improved in just a few days. Once balance is achieved, perform the exercises five to ten times.

Begin by standing with your hands resting on top of your head, palms together in prayer fashion.

Keeping the knees together, in a very slow motion, lower your body until the buttocks touch the heels. If you cannot go that low, do not be discouraged. Go as far down as is comfortable for you without strain. Keep your back straight. If you find that you lose your balance, spread your legs so that the knees are not as close together. When you reach your lowest point, do not pause!

Raise slowly up again, coming all of the way up onto your toes and hold for a count of five to ten. Then lower the soles so that the feet are flat and then repeat the exercise.

Remember to visualize and focus on your body as you warm up. Having performed the outer physical exercises, it is a good idea to do some internal exercises as well. The most important is breathing. At the end of your exercises, sit or stand and close your eyes. Begin performing deep breathing from the diaphragm. Slowly inhale for a count of four. Hold for a count of four, and then exhale slowly for a count of four. This kind of deep breathing will increase the oxygen supply in the blood and warm up the inner muscles and organs.

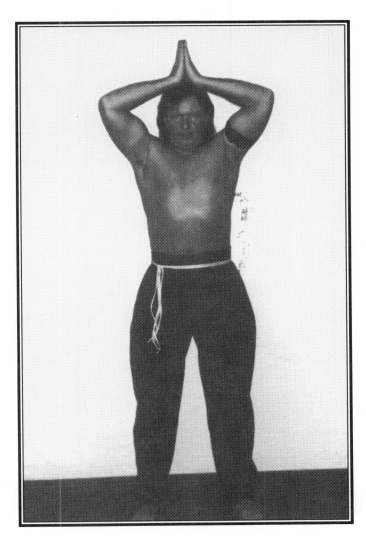

The Dancer's Exercise, figure 1

The Dancer's Exercise, figure 2

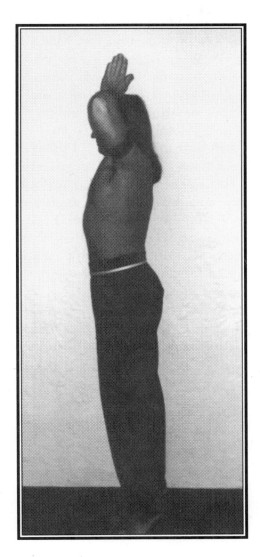

The Dancer's Exercise, figure 3

Magickal Dance Exercise:
Overcoming Inhibitions

Most people are self-conscious when it comes to dancing, especially in public. This holds true for magickal dance and ceremonial/ritual movement as well. Men particularly often have difficulty with their inhibitions. Dance in Western society has not really been sanctioned for men. Traditionally, western men express themselves through movement by participating in sports. Thus it is often more difficult for men to use dance as a tool for self-exploration and for magickal purposes. Barriers must be broken down.

For anyone self-conscious or inhibited about dance, it is important to dance several times a week to overcome self consciousness and shed inhibitions. Remember, it is not the ability but the participation which activates the energy. Through ceremonial dance, we learn to express ourselves. We fulfill an inner need to create.

Take time initially to learn to move freely. Learn to be comfortable with your body, its appearance, and its ability to move in the manner most natural for you. Most people love to dance but can't, either because they don't know how to begin, or because they are embarrassed. Usually we are uncomfortable because we have lost the natural confidence and rhythm of childhood. The following exercises will help you recapture that naturalness and help eliminate inhibitions:

1. The physical tools for dance are the steps or movements and the shapes or the forms we take. Most steps are simple and are movements most of us find familiar. Skipping, galloping, jumping, hopping, swirling, sliding, and walking are all movements that we used in play as we grew up. They are also intrinsic to dance.

    Find a time and a place where you can be alone. Find your favorite kind of music. At first, simply sit and listen to the music. Feel it penetrating you. Notice its rhythm. Now stand and begin jogging to the music.

    Jogging is natural. It's non-threatening because it's familiar. Through jogging we begin to combine music with movement, and we begin to break down barriers. Jog in a pattern you feel is good. You may wish to jog back and forth, in a circle, or in a zig-zag. Do whatever seems right for you.

After several minutes of this, change the music, and skip or jump to it. Then try galloping, sliding, and even walking to the music. Swing your arms to it. Shake and wave your arms. Clap if you feel the desire. No one is going to see you but you.

Mix the jogging with occasional jumps, slides, or skips. Notice how you introduce moves when they seem appropriate to you. You are freeing your creativity. After ten to fifteen minutes of this, you may find yourself laughing or giggling at yourself. You may even tell yourself that you are looking silly, but you will be smiling and laughing about it. Remember that dancing is joyful. It frees us.

2. Now take a piece of classical music—something slow and soft. Take a seated or reclining position on the floor. Close your eyes and allow yourself to absorb the music and its rhythm. As you do, raise your hands and allow them to dance and move to the music. Move only your hands and fingers, limit the movements of other parts of the body, including the forearms.

Next stand up and allow the entire arm to move to the music. Keep the rest of the body still. You may wish to close your eyes or you may even wish to observe yourself in a full length mirror if you have one available. Notice how the movement of the arms appears to extend and diminish the dance space.

Then allow just your shoulders to dance to the music. Let your arms rest at your sides and move your shoulders to the music. Do the same with your head, the trunk of your body, and your hips.

For the last two movements it is best to stand. With your trunk you may feel the movement is rather limited. But as you play with it, you will discover there is a wider range of movement than you originally anticipated.

While continuing to stand, dance only your legs to the music. Keep your trunk still and the balls of your feet flat on the floor. Again, you may feel restricted in your movements, but you will still find you are capable of "leg dancing" to the music.

Finally, allow your feet to dance to the music. You may find this easier by performing it while sitting in a chair. Let your toes and feet move to the music.

You are learning that the entire body is capable of dance expression. Alter this exercise by using different types of music. Pay attention to which parts of your body move easiest to which kinds of music. This can help you release energy more effectively. This will also have greater meaning when we explore the body as an instrument of power in the next chapter. This information also will aid you in imbuing your movement with greater magickal significance.

Having done this several times, you may wish to practice dancing the body parts in front of a mirror with no music. The effort and focus should be on smoothness and flow. Visualize the different body parts as if you were moving them under water—slowly and gracefully.

3. Now change the music again. Allow yourself to move and dance to the music in the manner you feel comfortable. Allow your arms and hips to sway freely. Don't worry if it doesn't look like something other dancers might do. Don't worry if you are not athletic. Simply try to be as graceful as you can.

    You may wish to dance and move unencumbered by clothes. Don't worry about your appearance. Regardless of age or condition, the human body is a magnificent and beautiful creation.

    You are learning to free yourself and your own natural ability to move and dance. As children, we could spin, leap, and dance freely. With this exercise, you are working to release that child. You are freeing your energies and loosening inhibitions which can block the flow of energy from the inner to the outer world.

    Doing this several times a week will help you become comfortable with your body, with movement, and with playing once more. Have fun with it. Dance is joyful and creative. Change the music from time to time. Go to a jazz number. Try rock and roll. Dance to a waltz or a favorite classical piece. Allow your movements to flow naturally with the music.

4. Begin to experiment. Think back on something that you are thankful for—a particular blessing, a special person, unexpected assistance you received, etc. Let it be anything that made you happy. Now pick a piece of music that reflects it.

   Don't worry if it is not truly accurate, just so it seems to convey the mood. Play the music, and as you do, dance that situation, reliving it in movement. Treat it like a form of make-believe. Be free and spontaneous. You are beginning to participate in dance ritual.

As you perform these exercises, in several weeks time, you will notice some specific differences. Your energy levels will increase. Your mood will be more positive. Do not be surprised when others comment on these positive changes. You will look forward to these *play* times. After all, when was the last time you let yourself go like a child? Your poise in all life situations will improve. You will also notice yourself handling outside, everyday activities with greater ease, grace, and strength. This is the magick of dance, manifesting our inner energies in the outer world.

Magickal Dance Exercise: Activating the Microcosm

We are each a microcosm of the universe. We have reflections of all the universal energies within us. By learning to activate them, we create a magickal existence.

Most movement creates spirals of energy. These spirals of energy will be explored more fully in Part Two of this book. In essence, the energy spirals around us, linking the earth and heaven. We become a bridge between the two.

In traditional dance training, the individual is taught basic positions. These body positions are basic to dance all over the world. The first five positions activate a spiral of energy that forms around the body and links it to the earth below and the heavens above. The number five, in traditional numerology, is the number of the microcosm, of the universe expressing itself through the human being.

These positions are effective to do periodically throughout the day, as they are energizing. Assuming these positions, especially the positions of feet in figures three, four, and five, helps strengthen us in tense situations and gives us greater energy. Often, when I am lecturing, I will stand in position three. This gives me a solid base of energy to draw on throughout the lecture or workshop. Then, as I gesture, speak, and move, that spiral of energy is drawn up and used to help touch and teach the audience more effectively.

Practice assuming the five following positions. Feel and sense the spiral of energy rise up as you move from one position to the next. Remember to visualize the spiral forming and drawing upward, encompassing and energizing your entire body.

1. In position one, the legs are turned out from the hips. The arms are in a long shallow curve, and the palms face inward. The head should be up and the shoulders back. This will enable the spiral of energy to rise strongly.

2. In position two, the feet are about shoulder width apart. Raise your arms slowly and smoothly to shoulder height. See and feel your body expanding and stretching. At this point, you are filling up two-dimensional space.

3. In position three, the arms are again lowered and one leg is placed in front of the other. The heel of one foot just crosses the ankle of the other. This initiates and activates the energy spiral for the creation of intersecting space and dimensions.

4. In position four, the spiral of energy is extended, pulled upward, and strengthened. The feet are separated a little more, by a distance that is comfortable for you to stretch and point the front foot forward. Point it forward and draw it back, heel to ankle. Feel the spiral draw up and soften as you do.

5. In position five, the spiral is pulled all the way up and tight around the entire body. The heel of the front foot is placed against the big toe of the back foot. With the arms raised and curved up, the spiral is drawn more tightly around the body. With the arms remaining in a shallow curve, the spiral rises, but more gently and not as tightly around the body.

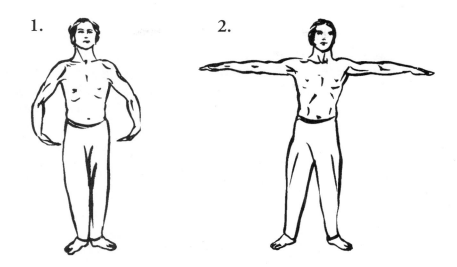

Creating a Spiral of Energy Through the Five Basic Positions

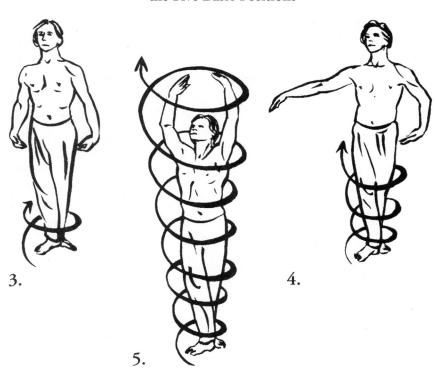

Experiment with these exercises. Pause after each position. Feel the energy and space around you as you do. Be aware of the spiral energy as it is activated and rises up and down. With practice you will learn to recognize it and control it whether you use these stances or the two more natural ones described below. Whichever you use, visualize yourself standing in the center of a vortex of energy, about to release it through the dance in a determined manner.

These ballet positions can be very unnatural to the untrained body. Turning the feet out can actually cause imbalance. A more natural way of standing for initiating dance in ritual and magick is by using an open stance, as in modern dance and in the martial arts. Two of these more natural stances are depicted in the photographs at the end of the chapter. These two positions will not change the magickal intent of the movement, rather they will reinforce the simplicity and ease of the ritual movement.

The first position is an open stance. One foot is placed straight forward and one is back and angled at no more than 45 degrees. They should not be on the same line with each other, but should be six inches to a shoulder's width apart.

The second is a simple parallel stance. Both feet are placed about shoulder-width apart, with toes directly straight. This activates a strong sense of balance and stability. With a slight angling, there is an ability to move with ease. Most often, the simpler and smoother the movements and postures are, the more effective they will be. Remember, the significance you give your movements is the most important aspect of magickal dance.

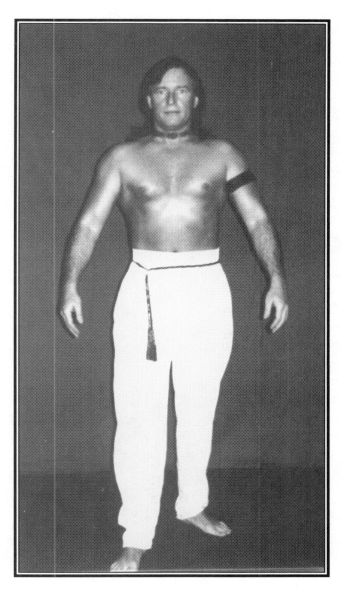

Initial Stances for Magickal Dance, figure 1

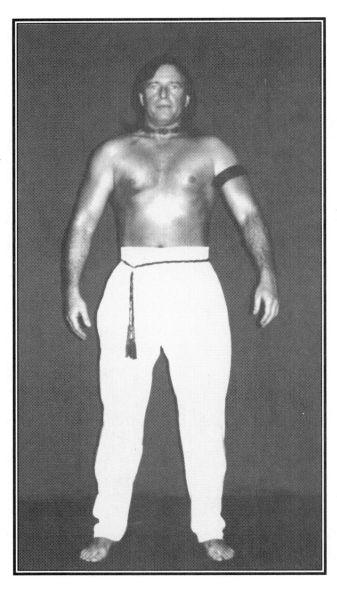

Initial Stances for Magickal Dance, figure 2

CHAPTER THREE

THE BODY AS AN INSTRUMENT OF POWER

To understand how movement and dance can create magickal changes, we need to see ourselves as an energy system. The ancients and modern scientists agree that everything in life is formed of vibration. That vibration is the result of the movement of the electrons and protons of every atom in every molecule of substance. Vibration exists in objects, animals, people, and in the atmosphere around us. The vibrational frequencies of animate life are more active, vibrant, and variant than inanimate matter, but vibration does exist in all.

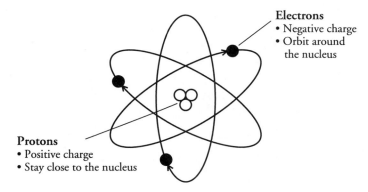

Electrons
• Negative charge
• Orbit around the nucleus

Protons
• Positive charge
• Stay close to the nucleus

The Energy Vibrations of Atoms

Energy Emanations of the Physical Body

The human body is comprised of many energy fields. These energy fields surround, emanate from, and interact with the physical body and mind. These fields include, but are not limited to, light, sound, electrical, thermal, magnetic and electromagnetic. They are scientifically measurable. One task of the modern metaphysical student and scientist is to determine which energies, intensities, and combinations are most effective for different processes—physical and spiritual.

When we run, the activity of the atoms increases, and there are corresponding physical physiological changes. The heart beats faster, the lungs work harder, circulation increases, and there are other changes. Some affect emotional and mental states. It is recognized that long distant runners experience a kind of euphoria. This is due partly to the release of endorphins by the brain during this sustained activity.

Because the human body is an energy system, we can use different energy forms to interact with that system. We can employ color, sound, fragrance, and even dance and movement to elicit specific changes in those energy vibrations. This can be done to increase intuition, to stimulate creativity, to induce deeper altered states of consciousness, to expand perception of the spiritual realm of life, and to heal.

With magickal dance we work to induce energy changes along specific avenues, and many of these are definable. We learn to recognize and direct very subtle, yet very real changes within our energy system by using movements.

Using the Occult Significance of the Body in Dance

Our body has much greater significance than what we often imagine. All energies upon the earth and those of the heavens play themselves out through it. Seeing the body as more than just a physical instrument that enables you to move around during the day is crucial to empowering yourself and especially your dance.

The body is a microcosm. It is a universe of energies unto itself. It reflects the greater energies of the universe, the macrocosm. When

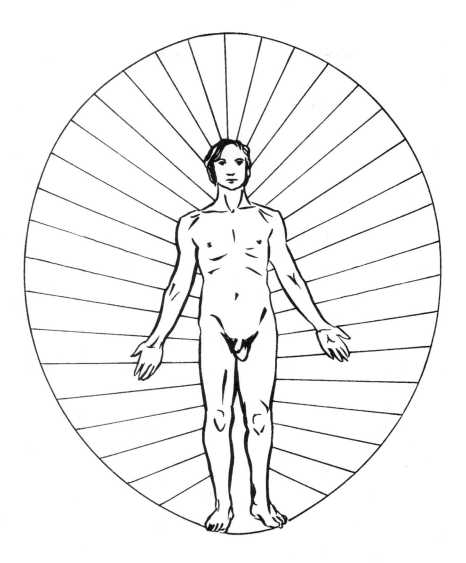

Energy Emanations of the Physical Body

There are a variety of energy fields that surround and emanate from the physical body. These fields include, but are not limited to, light, electrical, heat and thermal, sound, magnetic, and electro-magnetic. They are scientifically measurable and help to show that the human body is an energy system.

The Body as a Microcosm

Within the human body all of the energies of the universe, the heavens and the earth, play themselves out. As we learn to use the body in a more consciously directed manner, we open ourselves more fully to the universe, and we awaken and manifest its powers within ourselves and our lives. We become the living universe!

humans are called a microcosm, it should not infer that we are just a part of the universe, rather we are a miniature of the universe.

This means that our hands are not just instruments for grabbing and holding. Our legs are not just for standing and walking. Our hearts are not just for pumping blood. Every part of our body has a significance much greater than its physical responsibilities. They are instruments of greater power, a power and significance that is often hidden (occult). They are the points through which the energies of the universe flow—energies which can be manifested dynamically in our daily lives.

Our spirit has access to the entire universe and all of its forces. The physical form is an embodiment of our spirit. Thus, it must use the physical form to reconnect with those universal energies. It does so through the various organs, centers, and activities of the human body. Through magickal dance and movement, we awaken ourselves to the hidden forces which play upon our lives on subtle levels.

Heavenly Associations with the Body

PLANETS	PARTS OF BODY
SUN	Heart, back
MOON	Stomach, breasts, digestion
MERCURY	Hands, arms, nervous system, solar plexus
VENUS	Throat, voice, loins, veins, kidneys
MARS	Head, sex organs, muscular system
JUPITER	Hips, thighs, liver
SATURN	Skeletal system, knees, teeth
URANUS	Ankles, shins, cerebro-spinal system
NEPTUNE	Feet
PLUTO	Generative organs

SIGNS	PARTS OF BODY	SIGNS	PARTS OF BODY
ARIES	Head, face	LIBRA	Kidneys, ovaries
TAURUS	Neck, throat	SCORPIO	Sex organs
GEMINI	Hands, lungs	SAGITTARIUS	Hips, thighs
CANCER	Breasts, stomach	CAPRICORN	Knees
LEO	Heart	AQUARIUS	Ankles, calves
VIRGO	Intestines	PISCES	Feet

Some Occult Significances of the Body

BODY PART	SIGNIFICANCE
HEAD	Higher mind; place of heaven
EYES	Vision; clairvoyance; windows to the soul
MOUTH	Power of speech; the creative word; creativity and destruction
BONES	The support system; structure of the universe; seeds of life; resurrection
SKIN	Protection and higher sensory system; rebirth
ARMS	The ability to embrace and hold life experiences; activity
HANDS	Our tools for touching, caressing, and dealing with life experiences; giving and taking; symbolism varies according to position of the hand
LEGS	Our ability to progress and evolve; a symbol for lifting and raising oneself
FEET	Support and uprightness in movement
HEART	The seat of the soul; center of love and healing; the sun
BREASTS	Nurturing; mothering; nourishment
LUNGS	The ability to experience and enjoy life; freedom
STOMACH	Assimilation of experiences and ideas
SEX ORGANS	The creative life force; the perpetuation of life; the cosmic forces
HIPS/BUTTOCKS	Balancing; sexuality; power

Parts of the Body in Magickal Dance

The legs, hands, arms, and eyes are all powerful instruments in magickal dance. There are many ways of employing them for specific effects. We will touch on only a few, but they should be enough to give you a starting point. Remember that magickal dance is a creative process. Take these basics and create new ways of working with them for even more dynamic effects.

The Legs

The legs have a powerful significance. They represent our ability to progress and evolve. The fact that we can stand erect indicates much about our own evolutionary status in regard to other animals. The legs symbolize lifting and raising ourself higher.

In the previous two chapters we have seen ways of developing and activating the energies of balance and even creating the spiral of energy by proper positioning and movement of the leg. We can also use them as symbols for pillars in the Great Tree of Life.

The tree is an ancient and universal symbol, representing things that grow, fertility, and life. To some, it is the world axis, to others it is the world itself. Its roots are within the Earth and its upper branches extend toward the Heavens—bridging the two worlds.

Trees bear us nourishing fruit. They provide us with wood for the building of homes and the making of paper. As children, we climb trees, finding enjoyment in reaching new heights and new challenges.

Trees have always been imbued with certain magickal and spiritual attributes. Fairies and elves are believed by many to live in and around trees. Different trees have their own unique vibration, from the ash with its energy and symbolism of immortality, to the willow, whose energy can be used to heal aches and stimulate flexibility.

Assuming the position of the Tree of Life at the end of a ritual or meditation is a means of empowering it. The Tree of Life is an affirmation of the energies of the Heavens being channeled through you in your activities upon the Earth.

Stand with your legs firmly on the ground as depicted in the illustration. Place your feet about shoulder width apart. Imagine and

Becoming the Great Tree of Life

By assuming the position of the tree, we make ourselves a bridge between the Heavens and the Earth. We have our roots within the Earth while we reach toward Heaven. Concluding any ritual or exercise with this position activates the energies more dynamically.

feel as if roots are extending down through them, out the soles of your feet, and into the heart of the Earth. Feel yourself being anchored and attuned to all the Earth's energies and rhythms.

Now, slowly and deliberately, extend your arms up over your head. Visualize them as branches, extending up toward the stars. Imagine and feel yourself becoming the great Tree of Life, with your roots in the Earth and your upper branches in the Heavens. Feel the energies of both realms flowing through you and empowering you. Imagine and know that you will bear great fruit and will grow stronger and fuller each moment thereafter. You have become the Tree of Life!

The Hands

The hands are one of our most expressive tools. We can use them to grip and to release. We use them to caress and to fight. They are symbols for giving and taking. They reflect many of our physical, emotional, mental, and spiritual characteristics.

The sciences of Reflexology and Palmistry focus on the hand and its powerful characteristics. Reflexology, in part, involves understanding that there are points on the hand that are tied into every organ and system in the body. Most of the body's energy pathways, or meridians, terminate at the fingers. Palmistry is the study of what the shapes, lines, and mounds of the hands and fingers indicate about a person physically, emotionally, mentally, and spiritually.

Hand movements and gestures are important to magickal dance and are sometimes referred to as the true universal language. From signing for the deaf to the expressiveness of the hula dancer, the hands and fingers are a dynamic tool of communication with others and with higher aspects of our own consciousness. Learning to position the hands in various shapes and forms will activate certain kinds of energy patterns around us.

To the ancient Hermeticists, every action had a specific purpose and significance. Our hand gestures should have their own significance and should be associated with a specific dance. There should be no purposeless movement. The ancient practitioners of ritual and high magick used specific hand postures even when stationary. Refer to the chart, Dances for Hands and Fingers, for a few examples.

Sends love and protects.

Closes aura to outside influence.Calms and balances.

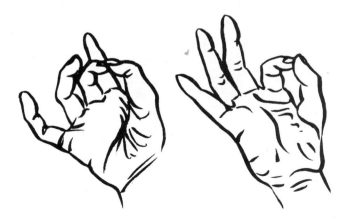

Activates specific energies during meditation.

Dances for Hands and Fingers

Fires energy outward.

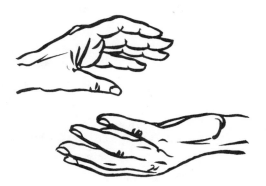

Palm Up—receptivity.
Palm Down—Activating and sending energy.

Strengthens, used to gain power.

Dances for Hands and Fingers

Positioning the palms of the hands is a simple and common way of directing energy in magickal dance. Three common hand postures in the Odissi temple dances were:

1. Palms up with the sides of the hands touching as if preparing to cup, a symbol of the yoni or feminine energies

2. A fist resting on the open palm of the other hand with the thumb of the fist pointing straight up, a symbol of the lingam or masculine energies

3. The hands in prayer position, a symbol of obedience to the higher.

In general, when the hands are held with palms up you become more receptive to outside energies. This position activates the feminine aspects within you—intuition, creative imagination, and illumination. The palms downward indicates more of an activating flow of energy. It stimulates the masculine aspects within you—the assertive, strengthening, and directing forces. Palms up activates form; palms down activates force. Form and force together, one palm up and the other down, creates a stress for growth.

When our palms are down, the energy radiates outward from the hands. When the palms are up, the energy is drawn in through the hands more easily. When alternated with one palm up and the other down, the flow of energy through and around the individual is balanced and more easily handled.

"Some Tantric teachers hide the meaning of their transmissions by making use of allegorical songs, riddles or coarse erotic rhymes, the true interpretation of which is only understood by initiates. Others use puns, mime, mystic gestures or secret signs. For example, if a Yogi shows one finger, it implies the question 'Am I welcome?' Stretching out two fingers in reply means 'You are welcome.' If a Tantric Yogi exhibits his fourth finger to a Yogini, she should indicate that she is proficient in the secret practices by stretching out her little finger; in this exchange of secret signs the Yogi and Yogini are affirming their mutual knowledge of the role of Heaven and Earth, while communicating their desire to perform practices together."[1]

[1] From *Sexual Secrets,* by Nik Douglas and Penny Slinger, (1979, p.148). Published by Destiny Books, a division of Inner Traditions International, Rochester, Vermont.

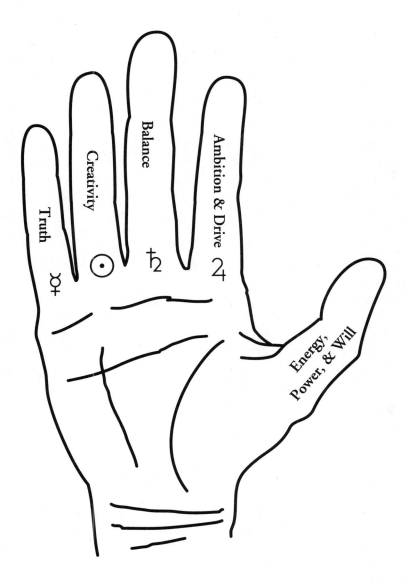

Energy Patterns of the Hand

Each finger on the hand represents a specific kind of energy pattern. Many groups teach that the thumb and one of the fingers should be placed together during meditation. This activates the energy pattern associated with the finger being used. The thumb strengthens the energy pattern. For example, joining the thumb and the middle finger releases an energy of balance.

Experiment with different hand movements and gestures. Feel the differences. Experiment with the way you hold your hands around other people. Pay attention to the way they respond. Our hands are tools for magickal communication.

The Eyes

There are powerful ways we can dance with our eyes. They have been called the windows of the soul, and they are symbolic of vision and power. Focusing the eyes on the tip of the nose stills the eyes and the mind. This allows vision to be turned inward, stimulating clairvoyance.

The eyes reflect and project inner states of energy. In Tantra, the four predominant gazes, or ways of using the eyes to direct energy, are petrifying, subduing, overthrowing, and conjuring. In the petrifying gaze, the eyes look toward the tip of the nose while the breath remains relaxed and motionless. In the subduing gaze, the eyes look to the left while the breath is inhaled. In the overthrowing gaze, the eyes are turned upward while the breath is exhaled. In the conjuring gaze, the two eyes are turned to the right and slightly upward while holding the breath. It is also a very seductive gaze.

Practice these gazes on people around you and watch their reactions. This will tell you much about the energy that can be directed by eye dances. Then try to incorporate them into your magickal dance ritual as well.

The Magickal Dance Attitudes

These positions are effective to use anywhere in your magickal dances to help you assimilate energy more effectively. These body positions can be assumed in the meditation itself after the introductory dance movements or at the end, before the closing dance movements. They help us to focus and release the raised energy so it can work for us.

Remember that these positions are guidelines. The important factor that we will stress throughout this book is to imbue every activity and posture with significance. Through the physical movements, gestures, and postures, we are learning to transcend the physical world to link with the spiritual world.

Variation on a Tantric Stance

In this position, there occurs a balancing and a controlling of the masculine force. Balancing upon one leg for overall balance and poise is combined with the mystical Tantric hand gesture which symbolizes the lingam, the male organ and masculine force.

Sitting or Resting

The first position is the *Sitting* or *Resting* position. This is a position of outer quiet with great inner activity. This activity is the result of the energy stimulated by the dance. The dance stimulates inner levels of consciousness. This position is representative of the changing energy from one state to the next. It is a position of closure and receptivity. It is especially effective for absorbing the energy patterns created and released through the dance.

Kneeling

The second physical attitude is that of *Kneeling*. This position, when done on both knees, represents the human ascent toward divinity while still attached to the earth. When assumed on one knee, it indicates an increase in freedom, a partial resurrection through the divine energies stimulated by the dance.

Prostrate

The *Prostrate* position grounds the energies activated by the dance. With outstretched arms, it becomes serpentine, as in the Serpent of Wisdom, which dances around the Tree of Life. The prostrate position can also be semi-prostrate, as in the yoga position of the cat stretch. In this, the arms are outstretched and the knees are tucked under the body. Womb-like in appearance, the dancer gives birth to new energies through the dance. It is a position of personal negation—an acceptance of divine authority. It is also an excellent position to use when reaching for the purpose or bindu at the center of your sacred space.

Standing

Standing is the fourth physical attitude. This position signifies that we are now able, through the energies we invoked, to be upright. We are now able to move. It signifies the emergence of light into the body and the manifestation of the magickal body. Both are accomplished through the energies of the dance. It is also symbolic of being able to move on to higher levels and achieve greater heights.

Take time and meditate upon each position while you are in it. Only as you use each position will you come to experience their greater significance in the dances of creation.

The Sitting Position—the position of closure and receptivity.

The Magickal Dance Attitudes

The Kneeling Position—the position of new ascent that is about to occur through the release of the dance energies.

The Prostrate Position—this is the position for personal negation and the acceptance of divine authority. It is the grounding of dance energies for the fulfillment of the purpose.

The Magickal Dance Attitudes

The Standing Position—the position
for the new ability to move to new
heights, reflecting the emergence of
the magickal body into physical manifestation.

The Magickal Dance Attitudes

The Immovable Posture

In Aikido, a form of Japanese martial arts, this posture is necessary for learning to breathe properly. Breath meditation (kokyu-ho) is essential to life.

In this position, the distance between the knees and from the knee to the foot is equal. The right big toe is crossed over the left big toe. The chin is in, the spine straight, and the individual sits solidly on the buttocks. This posture stabilizes one's energy, immovable here means imperturbable.

This posture shows how the magickal dance attitudes and postures can be combined for effects. It combines the sitting and kneeling positions.

CHAPTER FOUR

ELEMENTS OF
MAGICKAL DANCE

Dancing is a gesture of the whole body which allies the body with the soul. It is the becoming of energy—not just the becoming conscious of energy. Dancing induces electrical changes in the body, thus it induces specific states of consciousness. When we employ magickal dance, we are using purposeful physical behavior to activate real energies.

For dance to be magickal, we must learn to move with intent. Dancing compliments the intent and grounds our energy so that we can more fully experience it. We can then more easily integrate and apply it to aspects of our life.

Each hemisphere of the brain possesses its own abilities and each provides access to a force we can learn to use. When the two forces of hemispheres are integrated, they create a third force that we can access. It is a force that goes beyond personal expression by aligning our personal energies with the rhythms and forces of the universe. This force can be effectively manifested through dance.

Five Predominant Elements
of Magickal Dance

But for dance to work its magick, we must learn to employ five predominant elements—Centering, Balance, Posture and Gesture, Space, and Creative Imagination. They are fully described below.

Centering

Centering is the ability to activate, move, control, and direct energies around a central focal point. Most of the time, the energy is activated around us. We are the center of the universe. All the energies will play themselves out uniquely within our lives. Learning to maintain focus is crucial to employing magickal dance. If we are scattered in our focus, our movements will also be scattered. This, in turn, will bring chaotic and unpredictable energy into our lives.

Part of the centering process occurs by paying attention to the preliminary preparations of magickal dance ritual or meditation. This includes determining the theme and purpose of the dance, taking a ritual bath,and properly incorporating fragrance, music, and costume. All of these preparations help focus and center the mind and the movement for the greatest magickal effect. These preparations will be elaborated upon in chapter five.

Balance

Balance is not just an ability to stand posed on one leg without falling over. It is the relationship between the inner and outer. It is maintaining harmony and recognizing that the outer movement reflects the inner realities and that outer realities will affect inner movements.

View balance as a circle. There are outer and inner parts to the circle. Without one or the other, there is no circle, so there is no balance. This is why the circle and circle dances are so powerful and effective in ritual. They not only create a point of sacred space, but they also awaken a perception of inner and outer balance.

Balance is movement, it is active. We are constantly exposed to situations which test our ability to maintain balance. Dance forces us to move, shifting energies into new patterns, all within the circle of our temple, whether the temple is our body or an actual room. Magickal dance teaches us that if we forget to balance ourselves on any level, we fall down.

Posture and Gesture

Posture and gesture not only reveal our feelings, but they will produce them as well. This is especially important to understand when we apply posture and gesture for magickal and mystical purposes. If we have poor posture, we are unable to move and we become less flexible in our movements and in our thoughts.

Gestures not only reflect certain moods and energies but can activate them as well. Someone who stands with his or her arms folded across the chest is being very protective. Hands on the hips indicate a *show me* attitude. The palm of the hand held to the face expresses sympathy or concern, while curling that hand into a fist against the cheek indicates thoughtfulness.

Take a moment, close your eyes, and relax. Now place your fists on your hips and hold that position for thirty seconds to a minute. What are your mood and temperament like now? What does it make you think of? Now place the palm of your hand against the cheek? How does this make you feel? Do you notice that these gestures activate certain moods? Reading and studying books on body language will give you many ideas of how to incorporate gesture and posture into your magickal dance.

Space

Dance makes us aware of the *space* in which we move. Magickal dance doesn't require great space, nor should it. In part, magickal dance creates an illusion of great space, time, and power manifested within the area of your movement. Humans have a tendency to view things from a limited perspective. We rarely think about the space where we move and act out our lives.

Space is not just empty air. It is the element we move through, just as water is the tangible element that a fish moves through. Periodically, see yourself performing activities in the space around you as if the space was not just empty air but was a tangible element such as water. Walk across the room consciously, as if you are walking through water. Try to sense what the space feels like. As you learn to see yourself consciously moving through space, you open your perceptions to the more ethereal energies and beings that share that space with us.

Creative Imagination

Creative imagination is essential to opening the doors to spiritual energies and beings and should be used in conjunction with dance. Creative imagination is the ability of the mind to create images and scenes associated with a seed thought, purpose, or idea. You should visualize these images in a three-dimensional form.

Creative imagination, when used with dance, places the dancer into a scenario or essence that helps them release a specific kind of energy. This can be as simple as a visualization of the dancer in an ideal magickal image or body. It can also take the form of a highly concentrated daydream or actual dream, in which the individual becomes absorbed into the framework of the unfolding scenes. Through movement, the dancer is immersed in energy beyond the physical realm.

Dancing with creative imagination involves seeing yourself with the ability to touch all worlds through movement. You are the dancer at the gateway of all dimensions. With the right movements and visualizations you can enter and exit all of them.

Employing the creative imagination in dance facilitates our journey beyond the normal sensory world. We create a new awareness, a new kind of experience relating to this world. As we imbue our movements with proper imagery and significance, we empower them to gain entrance into the spiritual realms. We assume a union with those realms and find a new expression of soul power within our lives.

Outline to Dance Ritual and Meditation

As discussed earlier, centering is the ability to activate a focal point where energies can play themselves out more effectively in and upon us. Centering involves preparation and conscious effort by the magickal dancer.

Give yourself *time to prepare!* The amount of preparation time necessary will depend upon your purpose. If it is to be a meditation in which empowering movement is used, less preparation time may be necessary. If you are preparing for an elaborate ritual, involving a group of people, more time will be necessary to map out the moves. Remember that simpler is better. You do not need to have elaborate costumes and complicated movements to activate energy and force. Imbuing simple moves with great significance is all that is necessary to experience the dynamic effects.

Choose the *purpose* of your magickal dance. Will it be used for healing? For strength? To stimulate creativity? Will it be used as a prelude and conclusion to a meditation to empower it, or is it going to be the meditation itself? Decide what movements will most reflect your purpose. Take time to reflect on them and imbue them with as much significance as possible.

One of the simplest ways to learn magickal dance is to use it as a prelude to your regular meditation. It induces an altered state and helps create a shift in your perceptions. Use it at the end of the meditation to ground the energies and bring them into play in your life in a balanced manner.

Make an *outline* of your dance meditation. In it, write specifically what you will do and when you will do it. Begin by stating the purpose of your dance meditation. Then list the steps you will take throughout it. See the sample outline included in this chapter.

Determine any specific *aids* you can use to assist you in maintaining proper focus and a shift of consciousness. Aids can include fragrances, candles, costumes, or choosing appropriate music. They should assist you in the movements and in achieving the purpose of the meditation or ritual.

The Body of the Dance Ritual

As seen in the sample outline on the next page, the body of the dance ritual or meditation has three steps. The first step is the *Entering and Rending of the Veils*. This is the creation of sacred space in which new energy manifests itself according to the purpose of the ritual. The second is the *Balancing and Activating of the Magickal Dancer*. This involves balancing the newly created energies. The third step is performing the actual meditation. For a complete overview of a Dance Meditation, refer to the Sample Outline below.

Sample Outline of Dance Meditation

The purpose of today's meditation is _____.

I. PRELIMINARY PREPARATIONS

    A.   Prepare the temple or meditation area with fragrance and anything else you may need. You may include music, colors, crystals, stones, or anything that will help you focus on the particular energies you wish to activate. You should also do whatever is necessary to ensure your privacy.

    B.   Prepare yourself by bathing before the meditation. Performing a ritual bath helps to relax the mind and shift awareness away from the daily hassles and activities to an inner focal point. While lying in the bath, rehearse the movements and activation of energies in your mind.

II. THE BODY OF THE DANCE RITUAL AND MEDITATION

    A.   Movements for *Entering and Rending the Veils*.

    B.   Movements for balance and activation of the magickal body.

    C.   The actual meditation.

III. CONCLUSION OF THE DANCE RITUAL AND MEDITATION

    A.   Movements for balancing and absorbing the meditation energy.

    B.   Movements for *Closing the Veils and Exiting*.

Entering and Rending of the Veils

The circle is a very powerful symbol and motion, in both the physical and spiritual realms. It has no beginning and no end. It separates the inside from the outside.

Making or dancing a circle is an act of creation. It is the marking of sacred space. It creates a sacred space within the mind, a place between worlds, a point where the subtle and tangible can intersect and play. Marking off a circle in the Wiccan tradition is sometimes referred to as *raising a cone of power.* The circling creates an energy vortex that facilitates altered states of consciousness and the activation of energies according to the purpose and method of dancing. Methods of working with magickal circle dances will be explored more fully in chapter six.

The circle movement is a dynamic way to initiate any dance ritual or meditation. Prepare the area with fragrance, candles, or whatever else you feel is appropriate. Then, slowly and steadily circle the area in a clockwise motion. Place your feet solidly and steadily as you encircle the area you will be using. I recommend that the area be circled three times, as three is the rhythm and number of creativity. Different numbers of circulations will activate different patterns of energy. This also will be explored more fully in chapter six.

The center of the circle is a focal point. All dance is a series of movements around a central point, be it an altar, a fire, an individual, or an idea. Movement adds energy to that focal point—your purpose. Movement around a point of focus seals out extraneous energies that can interfere with the ultimate purpose of the ritual or meditation. As you encircle the area, focus on your purpose. See it growing stronger within the circle as you make your revolutions.

As you return to the point of origin, take three steps toward the center of the circle and bow. This is a traditional beginning. You are reverencing the creative energy and the sacred space you are activating.

Now extend your arms in front of you, with the backs of your hands touching. Then slowly and deliberately pull your arms apart until they extend straight out to your sides at shoulder height. This movement is like the peeling back of drapes or curtains. In this case, it is the rending of the veils between the physical and the spiritual.

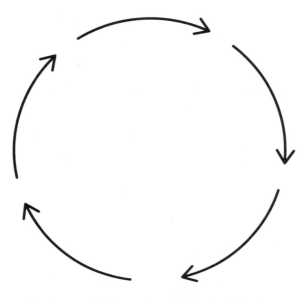

Encircle the meditation or ritual area in a clockwise direction to create sacred space. Take three steps into the center and bow.

While standing in the center of your sacred space, peel back the veils separating the physical realm from other realms of energy. Feel the energy fill the sacred space with its power and align with your individual purpose.

Entering and Rending the Veils

The circling creates a sacred space where we can more easily separate the veils between the worlds and opens a stronger flow of energy from the spiritual to the physical world. Remember to imbue this movement with as much significance as possible. Visualize and imagine that the veils separating other realms from ours are opened to reveal wonders and energies.

Take time to feel the effects of this motion. Allow the energies to fill the sacred space you have marked off, intermingling and infusing all within the circle with its power. See and feel your focal point becoming stronger and more tangible. Feel the process of manifestation beginning with these movements.

Balancing and Activating the Magickal Dancer

You have created a sacred space and opened the veils between the worlds. Now you must balance yourself with these new energies. Any new influx of energy must be balanced. Using the poses and positions in chapter one can be effective because they help focus the mind and create an easier shift in consciousness. Use these poses and positions at the end of your dance to ground the energies of the ritual and creates a stronger physical manifestation.

There are three exercise variations, all of which can be used to help stabilize and control this new energy. Do not be afraid to experiment and create your own variations. As you perform each exercise, see yourself taking on a magickal body with the power to manifest and direct energies to fulfill your meditation or ritual purpose.

The first variation is the *Hanged Man,* based loosely on the tarot card of the hanged man. In the tarot deck, the figure is hung upside down. In our variation, it is performed in an upright position. This is an exercise that will develop balance and a greater awareness of new perspectives. It will help make you more sensitive to the creative energies within your sacred space.

Begin by standing with both feet shoulder length apart. Take the foot of either leg, and slowly draw it up the opposite leg. Place it behind the knee of that leg. Hold your arms out or fold them across the chest. Hold this position as long as you can. See yourself balancing the new energies within the sacred circle.

The Hanged Man Pose

Begin by slowly drawing one foot up the side of the opposite leg. Place the foot behind the knee of that leg, and hold this position. Then lower and reverse feet and legs.

The Dancer Pose

Having balanced in the Hanged Man pose on both legs, move smoothly into the traditional Dancer's Pose. Visualize yourself in your magickal body, able to dance between worlds.

Now lower your foot and perform the movement with the other leg and hold it as well. Lower it and then move into the traditional dancer's pose as you learned in chapter one. By doing so, you not only balance the new energies in your sacred circle, you are also ready to direct them more fully toward the fulfillment of your meditation purpose.

As you assume the *Dancer's Pose*, visualize yourself in your magickal image or body. See yourself able to mold, shape and direct this new energy that has opened with the rending of the veil to manifest the goal and purpose of the meditation. See yourself as able to dance between the worlds.

The second variation, called the *Pillars of Balance*, is similar and extremely balancing. Often times, after performing some rituals and meditations, you may find yourself over sensitive and over energized. This exercise will stabilize those hyper-energies effectively.

See your legs as pillars. One leg represents the feminine energies and the other the masculine. If you are male, the dominant side will be the masculine and the other side will be the feminine. If you are female, the dominant side will be the feminine and the other will represent the masculine. The dominant side can be determined by whichever hand you use the most.

Stand with legs about shoulder width apart. Slowly raise one of the legs up so you are standing on one foot. Keep your eyes focused straight ahead. This will help you maintain balance. Hold this position as long as you can, at least thirty seconds to a minute. Then slowly lower the leg.

Reverse the position. Raise the opposite leg and hold this position. Lower this leg and then stand firmly with both legs flat and strong upon the ground. Raise your arms to the heavens and hold them there.

While performing this exercise, see your legs as pillars of strength and balance. Visualize and know that while you perform this, the male and female energies within you are balancing and strengthening. Whenever the male and female energies harmonize and join, new birth occurs.

Also, imagine as you extend your arms upward in the last position, you take upon yourself the energies and abilities of the magickal body with all of its power. See yourself in control of those energies

Pillars of Balance

As you learn to balance on each leg (pillar), you balance both sides of the brain. You also harmonize the feminine and masculine energies within you.

Pillars of Balance (continued)

As you assume a pose with both pillars on the ground and arms stretched to the heavens, you become magickal. You are the bridge between the worlds and the energies of the physical and the spiritual will be played out within you and through you.

within this sacred circle, and know that you are a link between them and their manifestation in your physical life.

You can use the last variation, *Moving Between the Worlds*, to balance your energies and set them in motion more dynamically in your physical life.

Stand straight, with your feet solidly upon the floor. See yourself standing firm and strong. Now rise up on your toes and hold the position. Then lower yourself into a squat position, remaining on your toes. Do not force the squat. Go down only as far as is comfortable for you. Keep your movements slow and deliberate.

By raising up on your toes and squatting up and down, you are drawing in new energies and setting them in motion inside you. You are working between the worlds that are manifest and worlds that are not.

These balancing exercises are effective to use by themselves just to maintain balance. If your daily life gets hectic and chaotic, take time at the end of the day and move through all of these dance postures and positions. Visualize your outer life becoming stabile and calm as you perform them. The results will surprise you. Within twenty-four hours, things will begin to settle down.

Using these poses periodically throughout the day helps you maintain and develop greater harmony and balance. As you increase your ability to stay balanced during these poses and exercises, you will also increase your ability to stay balanced in all avenues of life. You will find that your ability to direct and control those subtle spiritual energies will increase. What you develop on one level affects you on all others—everything affects and reflects everything else. That is especially important to remember in magickal dance.

Performing the Actual Meditation or Ritual

So far, you have created a sacred space, opened the veil, and balanced the flow of new energy into that space. Now the final part in the body of the dance ritual must be performed. This can be simply performing whatever meditation you have chosen, or it may involve dance movements that you have choreographed specifically for this ritual.

As you rise up on your toes and are able to balance, you are learning to draw in the new energy within the sacred circle. It also develops the ability to balance this new energy and more consciously direct it for your own purposes.

The slow, deliberate movements up and down develop and reflect your ability to apply this energy in both the physical and spiritual realms of life.

Moving Between the Worlds

Pause briefly after balancing yourself. Use a prayer, an affirmation, or a statement of purpose at this point. The vocalizing of the purpose is a dynamic way of centering new energy. Then move into the meditation itself. Assume a meditative pose or begin the dance that is specific to your purpose. There are some guidelines on different meditative poses and the kinds of energies they invoke in the next chapter. Aligning the pose with the purpose empowers the entire process.

Conclusion of the Dance Ritual or Meditation

In our sample outline of a dance meditation, the third and final part serves two functions. In the first part, use movement and posture to absorb energy activated by the meditation during the body of the dance ritual. The second part is to close the veils and dissipate the sacred circle of energy.

At the end of the meditation, visualize the energy of the circle accomplishing its purpose. See yourself stronger, healthier, and more balanced. See the circle creating and manifesting all that you envisioned.

Do not imagine it coming to you in the future. There is no future, and there is no past. There is only the present, that sacred intersection where what was and what will be meet. See, feel, and imagine things as if they had already occurred. Take time to reflect upon how the circle empowered you. If you wish, offer a prayer of thanksgiving and affirmation to reinforce your visualization

Perform a balancing exercise to help ground the energies into manifestation. Then stand and take three steps back from the center of your sacred space and bow. This is the traditional closing and should be done with reverence.

Extend your arms to your side, at shoulder height. The palms of the hands are facing front. Keeping the arms extended, draw them forward until the palms touch. Visualize this as a closing of the veils between the two worlds. Imagine that you are drawing drapes or curtains closed. Then fold your arms across your chest or place them in a prayer position at your chest. This pushes the ritual energy into place and grounds it into physical activity within you and your life.

Turn and encircle the meditation area slowly and deliberately, just as you did in the beginning, only this time move in a counterclockwise direction. The significance of the directions will be covered more fully in chapter six.

As you make your three revolutions, visualize the energy of the ritual being grounded into your physical life. See it taking effect immediately. Know that the purpose has been fulfilled. At the end of the revolutions, pause, breathe deeply, extinguish all candles, and go about your regular activities until you create that sacred space again.

Magickal Dance: The Sun and Moon Breath Dance

This meditative dance is taken partially from the oriental art of tai chi chuan and employs breathing techniques, called *the Sun and Moon Breaths*. This exercise will balance the hemispheres of the brain and will shorten study time. It heals and strengthens all systems of the body and is an effective tonic for recuperation after illnesses. It activates the heart chakra while balancing the male and female polarities of the body to stimulate creativity, fertility, and intuition.

1. Familiarize yourself with this exercise. Choose an incense or a color candle that is effective. Red and blue candles can be effective (red = masculine, blue = feminine). A rose fragrance is very effective.

2. Create your sacred space by encircling the area in a clockwise motion. Circle the area six times. We will use six as a predominant rhythm, because it is a number associated with the heart center.

3. Take three steps in toward the center and bow. Then open the veils between the worlds. Pause and feel the new energy filling the sacred space.

4. Use any of the balancing positions to harmonize yourself with this new energy.

At the end of the meditation, take three steps back from the center of the circle and bow. Then extend the arms out to the side, and with a deliberate drawing motion, bring the palms of the hands together or fold arms over chest. This movement serves to close the veils between the worlds.

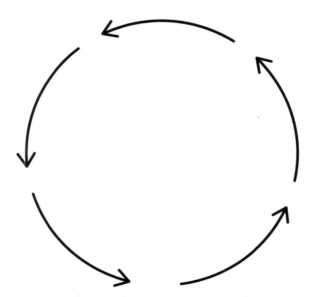

Encircle the meditation or ritual area in a counterclockwise motion. This dissipates the energy of the sacred space.

Closing the Veils and Exiting the Circle

5. The sun breath is a slow exhalation, extending the arms forward in front of the chest, with the palms facing outward. By exhaling audibly, the energy level is increased. We are pushing the energy of the inner sun out into the aural field. The moon breath is the inhalation, drawing the arms and the energy into you with the palms facing inward.

6. On the inhalation, always bring both hands back to the heart area. Take a few moments and practice both before using it in the meditation form. You will feel the energy moving out from you and drawing in through you. During the dance ritual, we will radiate this energy in six directions: forward, up, down, both sides, and the diagonals. It is performed using moves a – f:

   a. Raise the arms up, pushing energy up, and out. Draw the arms back, inhaling and bringing the hands back to the heart.

   b. Now push the arms and the energy down in front of the body, and then draw them back to the heart.

   c. Next, the right arm is extended out to the right and the left arm is extended at the same time to the left. Inhale and bring both arms back to the heart area.

   d. Now the arms are moved in a diagonal direction with the breathing. Let one arm push the energy up at a diagonal while the other pushes down at a diagonal. Draw them back together at the heart.

   e. Then reverse the positions of the diagonals. The arm that moved down at a diagonal will now move in an upward, diagonal direction. The one that moved down will now move up. Move the arms in unison.

   f. Finally, the arms are extended together in front of the body. Feel and see the sun inside you burst into brilliant light that radiates out in all directions around you. Draw the arms back with the hands together against the heart.

7. Take a few moments and feel the energy alive and vibrant in and around you. See yourself as energized, healthy, and strong. Offer a prayer of thanksgiving or an affirmation.

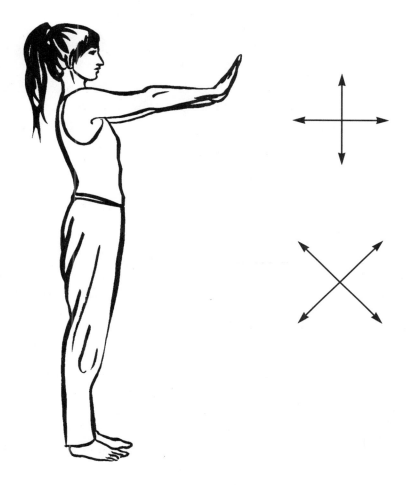

The Sun and Moon Breath Dance

As you exhale, slowly push your arms out in front of you. Now turn the palms toward you, and as you inhale draw your arms slowly back and fold them across your heart. Then repeat this movement up and down.

Next, the right arm is extended to the right and the left to the left, then drawn back together at the heart area. Then with the arms moving in unison, push one arm up at a diagonal and one down at a diagonal. Then repeat in the opposite directions. See yourself as the Sun, radiating in all directions about you.

everal deep breaths, then perform one of the balanc-
rcises so the energy you activate will manifest itself
_iously.

9. Take three steps back from the center of the circle and perform the closing of the veils between the worlds.

10. Turn and encircle the ritual area deliberately in a counterclockwise direction. This will dissipate the energy and close down the sacred circle. Make six revolutions, as you did in the beginning.

Magickal Dance: The Tibetan Walk to Nowhere

The *Tibetan Walk to Nowhere* is a series of steps that will induce an altered state of consciousness. It can help shift your consciousness away from the daily hassles, and it will help activate your higher intuition and clairvoyance. This dance stimulates our inner vision and creativity. Use it with visualization and creative imagination to move past obstacles that you encounter in any path of your life. It can be adapted to walk you into higher perceptions along any avenue of life you choose.

1. Decide what kind of perception you wish to walk into. In the beginning, I suggest you just walk to awaken your intuition and your own clairvoyant ability.

2. Choose an incense that is conducive to your purpose. Use a white candle initially, but you will find that other color candles will facilitate different kinds of walks.

3. Mark off your sacred space by encircling the meditation area three times.

4. Take three steps toward the center of this circle and perform the *Rending of the Veil* movements. Pause and allow yourself to feel and experience the influx of new energy in your sacred circle as the veils are opened.

5. Perform one or more of the balancing exercises, to stabilize yourself and your energy system.

6. Now begin the *Tibetan Walk to Nowhere*. This walk involves a repetition of a pattern of steps. It involves four steps forward and four steps back. Four steps forward and four steps back. Forward, back. Inner, outer.

   The steps should be taken in a sure, slow, and deliberate manner with full attention upon them. Place the heel down first and then the toes with each step. This serves as a reminder to maintain sure footing in all of your spiritual journeys and especially upon the path you are now treading.

   Your hands can be folded in a prayer position at the chest, or crossed at the heart with a hand upon each shoulder. Visualize yourself in your magickal body as you perform it. In time you can visualize yourself walking upon a path of a particular color, a color appropriate to your purpose. For example, use a red path for strength or a green path for growth.

   Perform this walk for at least five minutes. See and feel yourself growing stronger in the energy of your purpose with each step. After five to ten minutes, pause and either continue standing or sit down, whichever is most comfortable for you.

   Take time to feel and experience the energy around you. What do you sense? What do you see in your mind's eye? Allow the energy to be absorbed back into you, knowing it will grow stronger each day thereafter.

7. Perform your balancing movements to stabilize this energy so you can express it more effectively in the outer world. Offer a prayer of thanksgiving or do an affirmation.

8. Take three steps back from the center and perform the *Closing of the Veils*.

9. Turn and encircle the ritual area three times in a counterclockwise motion. This will dissipate the energy and close down the sacred circle until it is needed again.

The Key to Magick in Movement

The key element to create magical movement is to imbue the moves and postures with great significance. This awakens and concentrates the inner energy you wish to release through magickal dance.

The Key to Magick in Movement

All traditions had a means of using movement to invoke and manifest this dynamic universal energy. In Eastern traditions, it is the power of the kundalini that is awakened through yoga. In the ancient Hawaiian tradition of Huna, it is called mana. In the orient, it is called chi or ki, developed most often through the martial arts. This inner magickal energy is called psychic energy or life force by modern metaphysicians. Every mystical tradition combined and used all five elements for the greatest magickal effects through dance and movement.

Chapter Five

The Power of Imitation

One of the most common forms of sacred and magickal dance was the imitation of nature and the life within it. Individuals would perform the dances of various animals to align themselves with the animal's power and awaken this power within his or her life.

In more ancient times, shamans were the keepers of the sacred knowledge. They were held in high esteem and recognized as true shapeshifters. They would employ dance to tie themselves to specific rhythms and forces of nature.

Shamanism is an experiential growth process. Through techniques utilizing magickal dance and costume, the shaman is able to visit the sky and the underworld. The shaman aligns with the energies of the Earth and learns from all life forms.

A prevalent symbol for shamanism, the Masked Sorcerer, is shown in this chapter. The image is taken from a prehistoric cave painting. Early humans, surrounded by mysterious forces, responded to them through imitation. They tried to bring the divine into accord with humanity. Priests and priestesses used totems and images to assist them in coming face to face with this mystery. Through dance, costume, and ritual, the priest or priestess would share the deity's identity and it's powers.

Part of the shamanic tradition involves re-connecting to the energies of the Earth and the life upon it. Animal imagery and sacred dance are used to assist with this re-connection.

All forms and images, including animals, reflect a manifestation of archetypal energies. We do not have to believe that these animals are beings of great intelligence, but there is a power, an archetype, that resides behind and oversees these life forms. These archetypes have their own qualities and characteristics which are reflected through and symbolized by the behaviors and activities of the animal.

When we honor the animal through sacred dance, we are honoring and invoking the essence that lies behind it. This essence is both creative and dynamic, and it can enhance our own life circumstances. When we open a sacred space and then attune to that essence through dance, movement, and posture, we share in its energy and manifest it within our own lives.

The animal becomes our totem—our power or medicine. It is a symbol of a specific kind of energy that we are invoking and using in our life. When we take on the image of the animal and dance its movements, we release the archetypal energies behind them into our lives.

Each species of animal has its own characteristics and the ability to remind us of the infinite power we can manifest in our own lives. By aligning and dancing to them, we are awakened to the the realities of the natural and what we now call the supernatural.

Through dance we learn to shapeshift our energy into a pattern similar to the energy of our totem animal. Developing this shapeshifting ability teaches us that we can re-create our lives. It shows us how to walk in harmony with all environs and in all worlds visible and invisible. It illustrates to us that we are not truly separate from anything upon the earth and that we can bridge the natural and supernatural realms.

A totem is any natural being or animal to whose energy we feel closely associated and can relate to within our life. The most powerful are those of the animal kingdom. Some totems reflect energies operating for only short periods in our life, and some are with us from birth to death and beyond. They are symbols for the expression and transformation of energies, stimulating our creative forces.

There was a time when humanity recognized it was a part of nature and that humanity and nature were inseparable realities. The

The Masked Sorcerer

This is the symbol of the prophet, the medicine person and the manifestation of the powers of nature. Images such as this invoke a presence which helps the individual to transcend the physical. Wearing the skins of the animal was a means of appeasing its spirit and honoring its power.

natural and the supernatural merged and blended. People used nature symbols to express and strengthen this unity. These symbols were often employed in sacred dance to re-instill a transpersonal kind of experience. This could involve the carrying or wearing of certain feathers or animal skins, creating a headdress of deer antlers, or holding flowers and crystals throughout the dance.

A fetish is an object regarded as being the embodiment or the habitation of a potent spirit. It is the object that ties us to the specific archetypal totem force we are trying to awaken and invoke through the dance. They are symbols of the natural forces of nature. These symbols can be feathers of a particular bird to which you are drawn, a headdress of deer antlers, a crystal or stone, and even an herb or flower. They are anything that helps to tie you to the energies of your totem.

The fetish use is most recognizable in the Kachinas of the Southwest. All Pueblo Indian tribes had Kachinas, but the Hopis and the Zunis have the largest number. They are not gods themselves, but they are representations in human form of the spirits of plants, animals, and birds. The Kachina dancer is believed to receive a spirit when the mask with its fetishes is worn. The dancer then becomes a mediator between the prayers of the village and the deity or natural force.

Adopting the movements and guise of nature in dance is a way of re-awakening primordial wisdom in ourselves. The fetishes we employ in the dance represent the totem force we wish to invoke. They, along with the dance movements, are symbols of the energy and creativity we wish to manifest. They help us to shapeshift our normal consciousness to a stronger alignment, perception, and consciousness of that particular force of nature. The alignment is invoked through the dance so it may fulfill a particular purpose for a dancer.

Shapeshifting Through Magickal Dance

The first step is to determine what your animal totem might be. Some meditation techniques can help us identify them, but one of the easiest is to simply begin with the animal or animals that have interested you the most.

The Eagle Dancer

Costumes and movements are employed to awaken the archetypal force behind various animals. Eagle dances were employed by many groups of people. The eagle is a powerful totem because it soars out of sight. It is believed to have a close relationship with the sun and its power is often sought in healing. Including feathers in the costume, along with the mimicking the movements of flight, help manifest its energy. Different feathers are symbols of different qualities of energies of the eagle. Flight feathers are for strength and fluff feathers symbolize the breath of life.

Which animal or bird has always fascinated you? When you visit a zoo, which animal do you wish to visit first? What animal or animals do you see most frequently when you are out in nature? Of all the animals in the world, which are you most interested in? Do you often dream about a specific kind of animal? Are there animal dreams that you have never forgotten? Have you ever had encounters with animals in the wild? Answering these kinds of questions provides strong clues to which animals are likely to be totems for you.

Once you have determined the animal, begin a closer study of it. Go to your library and examine books and films about this animal. Notice the way it moves, the way it stands. How does it hold its head? How does it place its feet when it walks? Then pantomime those same postures and movements.

Most of the ancient sacred animal dances were developed by simply mimicking and imitating animal forms and postures. Study some of the Eastern sciences such as yoga or Kung Fu. Many of the movements are based upon animal movements. There are many books which depict these postures. This can give you a starting point in which to build your own dance. Some examples are shown in this chapter to help you get started.

Dancing and movement for shapeshifting involves more than transforming oneself into a beast. This is not going to happen, at least not in the physical realm. As we learn to use dance, we can change the form in which we appear on other planes, this in turn will affect us on the physical plane. Most of the ancient tales of shapeshifting were either symbolic or reflected a time in human evolvement when we were not so grounded in physical energies. Shapeshifting dances, as we will learn, will help you align and manifest the power of the totem animal more strongly within your present physical form and life. The following steps can be used as a guide to shapeshift through magickal dance.

1.   Begin by determining and researching your totem. Find pictures, make collages, look for things that can represent it to you. Use some of the guidelines in chapter six to help you develop a costume that will assist you in attuning and synchronizing with the energy of your totem.

2. Next decide on three to four basic moves which reflect the energy of this totem you wish to incorporate within your own life. Practice mimicking and pantomiming its movements and postures.

3. Take time to meditate upon this animal. Visualize and imagine it as a spiritual companion wherever you go. Visualize and imagine its energy coming alive within you and enabling you to accomplish specific goals.

4. In the center of your dance area, place any fetishes, pictures, costumes, or other items that will serve to align you with your totem. If you wish, you may already be dressed and prepared. Do what works best for you.

5. Begin your shapeshifting dance by marking off the sacred space. Encircle your dance area three times. Then take three steps toward the center and perform *the Rending of the Veils*. Pause and allow yourself to feel and experience the energies of the physical and the spiritual worlds blending and merging. Feel this new influx of energy.

6. Put on your costume slowly and deliberately. Imagine that this new energy is transforming you into your totem. See, feel, and imagine your totem appearing in the circle with you.

7. Perform the balancing exercises to stabilize yourself with these new energies.

8. Now, begin the movements and postures associated with your totem. As you take the stances and make your steps around the circle pantomiming and imitating this power animal, feel it coming alive within you. You may even wish to act out how you will use this power successfully in your daily life. See yourself manifesting it creatively and productively. Know that you have aligned yourself with its essence.

9. Now assume one of the physical attitudes described in the last chapter—sitting, kneeling, prostrate, or standing. Hold the position like you know your totem would. If your totem is a bird, stand like that bird. If it is an animal, you may wish to lay

prostrate as that animal would. Be creative. Absorb the energies of the circle while holding this pose, and then perform the balancing exercises again.

10. Remove the costume, knowing that the outer form and the energies it represents are now alive within you.

11. Take three steps back from the center, and perform *the Closing of the Veils*.

12. Encircle the area in a counterclockwise motion three times to dissipate the energy of the sacred space and to return the environment back to normal.

Important Precautions in Shapeshifing

Be flexible in these steps. Experiment with them and adapt them to find what works best for you. Dance and shapeshifting are creative processes. We can give you the basic formulas and ideas, but for them to become truly magickal you must apply your own creative imagination and intuition.

Of course, there are precautions necessary in any kind of shapeshifting work, especially when done through dance. The effects of dance rituals are often not very subtle. The dancer should be prepared for dramatic physical responses and releases. Initially, it is best that the taking on of totem aspects be done under the supervision of a knowledgeable and responsible priest or priestess.

Even though the dancer may not change physically to other observers, internally he or she may have a profound transformation and believe it has occurred physically. This should not be treated casually or lightly dismissed. Time and care must be used in assimilating and balancing the energies released through dance.

For the beginner, it is best to work with simple movements and postures before attempting ecstatic dance states. If you are not sure of your own ability to control and handle the energy activated through the dance, do not use it. No dancer should ever be allowed to continue dancing until they are exhausted. This is unhealthy and very damaging to the energy field of the individual.

Many shamanic techniques involve using the drum to induce the altered state and facilitate the shapeshifting. The drum can also be used to draw the individual back into reality. One drum technique involves using a slow, heartbeat-like rhythm and then building in intensity to release the consciousness and facilitate the transition. Reversing this and moving from the frenzied rhythm back to the heart-beat-like rhythm will draw the consciousness back to normal. This is especially effective because the individual does not then move from the deeply altered state to normal consciousness too abruptly.

Taking the hands of the individual and performing joint deep breathing assists in grounding the individual back into reality. Massaging the feet to open and activate the chakras that connect us to the earth and its reality will also assist. Sitting or laying prone on the floor while accompanied by the removal of any fetishes or costumes used in the transformation will facilitate this grounding process.

It is also beneficial to stroke the spine downward from the crown of the head. This stabilizes the chakras and draws the consciousness back into present reality. Remember that part of the goal is to develop conscious control and awareness through movement.

Some Magickal Animal Postures

The Cobra

Snake dances are universal. They were performed to activate the kundalini—the creative life force, to stimulate a shedding of the old and to initiate resurrection and rebirth. The serpent is the serpent of higher knowledge and wisdom.

The posture depicted on the next page is the *Cobra Posture* of Eastern Yoga. To perform it, lie flat upon the ground, face down. See yourself as a snake. Slowly lift your head to see more clearly, to raise yourself higher. Place your elbows under you, pushing yourself up even higher. Finally, with your head back, looking up as high as possible, stretch your arms out straight and hold the position of the cobra.

See and feel yourself as the great serpent of knowledge. See yourself opening to new sight and new birth with this movement.

The Cobra Posture

Snakes and serpents are ancient symbols of eternal wisdom and the higher creative forces of life. They represent birth, death and rebirth as depicted in the shedding of their skins. Performing snake or serpent dances and postures initiates an energy of rebirth and higher illumination.

The Butterfly

These movements reflect the emergence of the butterfly from the cocoon. The butterfly is a symbol of resurrection, of coming into new life. It brings beauty and light into this new life. If we wish to make our lives magickal, we must learn to emerge from the cocoon of old perceptions. The totem and dance movements will assist you in attaining new perceptions.

In the first position, bend over and hold onto your feet. This is symbolic of being wrapped in the cocoon of physical life and perception. While holding this position, begin to squirm slowly and deliberately. See yourself as a caterpillar that is beginning its metamorphosis into a butterfly.

In the second posture, you become the butterfly. Raise your head and draw your arms back from your feet. See and feel your arms as radiant wings.

At this point you can rise from the floor into your new life. Spin about, and see this spinning motion as lifting you lightly from your feet. Feel yourself as light and free. Notice the wings of rainbow light. Notice how your wings move with your thoughts. Allow yourself to fly about, hovering over flowers, trees, and people.

See and feel yourself as the magickal butterfly that flies out to enjoy the nectar of life. Let this nectar represent a goal, purpose, or desire within your own life circumstances. Taste it and savor it!

The Cat Stance

Cats are ancient, powerful symbols of magic and mysticism. They have been dynamic symbols of immortality—nine lives and such. In Egypt, it was associated with the moon and thus the feminine energies of intuition and instinct. Different cats are symbols of different variations of these energies. A study of specific cats will help you identify their unique powers.

This is a position taken from traditional Kung Fu. A cat is light on its feet, often walking on its toes. It is stealthy and silent in its movements. It is assured, steady and strong. The hand positions demonstrate in this chapter for the leopard and the tiger can be used in conjunction with this stance.

The Butterfly

These postures and movements activate the archetypal energies of new birth. It stimulates and creates opportunities for breaking free of the old cocoons and emerging into new energies and new life.

The Cat Stance

Cat stances and movements activate energy for greater confidence and sure-footedness in life. They can be used in ritual dances to create opportunities to get back on our feet.

Practice prancing surefootedly and softly within your circle. Know that as you become the cat, you become more surefooted in life. Know that you will live through anything that you feel is overwhelming you at the moment. In fact, performing cat dancing and postures helps create opportunities that put you back on your feet again.

The Crane

The crane has been esteemed for its majesty and grace. In Chinese and Mediterranean cultures, it has been a symbol of justice, longevity, and the abiding soul. It has also been considered a messenger of the gods, a mediator between heaven and earth. Its massive wingspan—up to eight feet—gives it great power of flight. It was believed to carry souls to Paradise and to the underworld.

This martial arts posture activates this same energy. It creates balance and strength. All kicks in Kung Fu involve this stance at some level. Learning to move and hop from one leg to the other gracefully will help you traverse the physical and spiritual realms gracefully. This posture activates intuition and greater discernment in working and walking between worlds and dimensions.

Animal Hand Gestures

Part of what we can learn from the martial arts is the ability to mimic animal gestures with the hands. In the Ninja tradition when held and used properly, the hands are points where the intrinsic forces of nature can manifest themselves.

The animal hand gestures can be incorporated into dance movements for shapeshifting. These are by no means the only gestures and positions, they are only presented to give you ideas to build on for your own totem dance.

The *leopard fist*, as shown in the illustration, helps develop strong and fast responses. A leopard uses quick, short movements. It is symbolic of valor and has been associated with Dionysus. The leopard fist is formed by folding the fingers halfway down with the thumb tucked in at the side.

The *ram's head fist* is a gesture of power. Any fist position activates the energy of strength and power. The ram is strong and sure-footed

The Crane Stance

The crane is a dynamic symbol of poise and balance. Working with its posture and movements will assist you in opening other dimensions and worlds with balance and strength. It can open the realms of the higher heavens or those of souls who have passed from physical life.

The Leopard's Fist

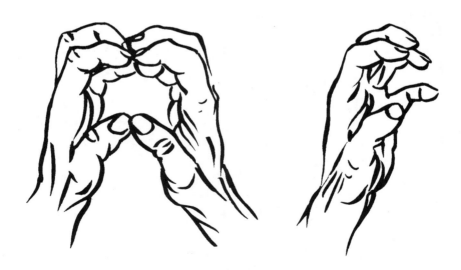

The Tiger's Claw

and has been the symbol of many kings in the past. It is a symbol of masculine fertility and strength and the creative impulse. To form it, the fist is turned slightly so that the first two knuckles are in front of the others. These two knuckles symbolize the horns of the great ram.

The *tiger's claw* gesture is also powerful and significant. It is known for its ferocity and strength. It has also been associated with the sun and the new moon. In its usual posture, the hand is tensed tightly and the fingers are turned inward.

To strengthen and imbue the body with greater energy, the finger tips are pressed together as hard as you can for a count of ten. Most of the major meridians or energy pathways in the body culminate at the fingertips. By pressing the fingertips together, all of them are stimulated, sending energy throughout the body.

Dragons are symbols of great power, strength, healing, and protection. In the orient, dragons have an ancient and tremendous mythology and they were often the symbols of emperors. Even though they are considered mythical, they also can be used as a totem.

The *dragon hand* has two forms. In the first, the knuckle of the middle finger is extended forward just little. It is the powerful head of the dragon. The claw of the dragon is formed by spreading all five fingers, and then bending and tightening the tips.

The *eye of the phoenix* hand can be used in dances for resurrection and for rebirth in times of trauma. It can be used to help create new opportunities from seeming losses through ritual dance. The phoenix rose from the ashes; shapeshifting into its form activates that same energy in your life.

The *eye of the phoenix* hand is formed by extending the knuckle of the index finger forward a little, as depicted in the illustration. Holding your hands in this position imbues the spirit with the ability to try again and again.

The *crane hand* can be used with the crane stance. It helps activate the dynamic and strong energies of this totem even more. The hand position mimics the long slender beak which can peck and hook fiercely and quickly.

The Ram's Head Fist

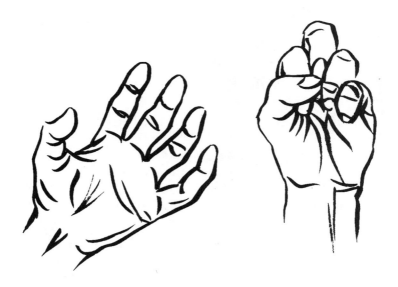

The Dragon Hands

The Eye of the Phoenix

The Crane Hand

White Snake Hand

The last sample is called the *white snake hand*. In Kung Fu, it is sometimes called the poison hand. It can be used in all serpent dances and with the cobra postures. The snake is fast and accurate when it strikes. The strike of some snakes has been timed at 100 miles per hour. This hand position helps awaken greater energy for speed and accuracy in handling life and for taking advantage of new opportunities. Snake dances, using just the hands, can create quick and sudden opportunities for transformation.

Dance Imitation and Shapeshifing, figure 1

By imitating the posture and movement of a tiger we help align ourselves with its energy. This energy is the archetypal force symbolized by the totem. It is its medicine that we are awakening and invoking into our own life for our own particular purposes.

Dance Imitation and Shapeshifing, figure 2

The cobra position of traditional yoga is effective in dance and movement to awaken the serpentine energy of primal wisdom. We invite the energy of the totem to play more dynamically and tangibly within our own life. All snakes represent wisdom and the cycle of birth, death, and rebirth. Using serpent dances or postures initiates this higher illumination.

CHAPTER SIX

THE THEATRE OF
MAGICKAL DANCE

With practice and a little imagination, you can choreograph an entire imaginary dance scene. It is a dance meditation done through pantomime. In many ways, this is similar to the mystery plays of more ancient times. The ritual enactment of specific energies and scenes releases their corresponding energies to the participants, linking the participants to the spiritual essences more effectively. These kinds of enactments can be performed by an individual or a group.

There must be messages and focus hidden within the movements. The dance is to become the teacher, and we allow the movement to communicate with us. Our higher levels of consciousness communicate to us through symbols. If we wish to strengthen that communication, we must make it two way.

This is where role-playing and pantomime are beneficial to magickal dance. Role-playing activates physical energy to give impetus to what we are trying to set in motion. We use the movement and the role to trigger other levels of consciousness more strongly.

In magickal pantomime, we will use the sacred space that we create to act out a situation with movement and gesture. We all play-acted when we were children, now we are going to do it in specifically controlled ways to release an archetypal force into our life.

You may feel silly at first, but that will pass. We are simply breaking down barriers that block the flow of creative energy into our lives.
When we were children, we could act out anything. We could make-
believe, and we got caught up in the reality of that play. We are using
this same process now, only we are infusing it with symbols and movements that will trigger specific manifestations. We are using this in a
controlled, concentrated manner to create new conditions, perceptions, and opportunities for new conditions in our physical life. The
steps to this magickal pantomime are simple.

1. Choose a subject matter for your dance, a focal point. This can
    be based on whatever you hope to accomplish with the ener-
    gies you set in motion. It can be anything from overcoming an
    obstacle to creating a new job opportunity.

2. Act out the subject for your dance. Act out whatever you are
    wishing to successfully accomplish. Practice it several times.

3. Now meditate upon your goal. Create an adventure narrative
    that reflects you accomplishing your purpose. You can con-
    struct it as you literally would like, or you can create an alle-
    gory for it. For example, you can create a magickal dance
    pantomime to overcome specific problems. The problem or
    obstacle can be depicted as an actual confrontation and over-
    coming of that specific problem, or it can be depicted in dance
    as in the fighting and overcoming of a dragon or beast.

4. What could you use to symbolize the other people involved or
    that which you are hoping to achieve? If it is, for example, the
    manifesting of a new job, see this as a treasure, a golden fleece,
    a Grail quest, or anything you like. Use the *Tibetan Walk to
    Nowhere* to lead you to this reward or new opportunity. Look-
    ing for ways of symbolizing the physical is a way of concen-
    trating energy around your focal point and empowering your
    dance.

5. Take this narrative and construct several movements, postures,
    and gestures that reflect its major activities. Be as simple or as
    intricate as you wish. A magickal pantomime for overcoming
    an obstacle can be depicted simply in three postures. The first
    could be one that reflects preparedness, standing strong and

confident. The second could reflect a confrontation and the third could be a posture of reception of the reward that will be yours for having overcome the obstacle. It can also be an elaborate sequence with a pantomime of everything done and felt from preparing to the overcoming.

6. Practice these movements. Don't worry that they may not be exactly what you would like. If you imbue them with significance, they will work. Have fun! Remember this is a creative process. Think of this as a powerful play time that you have denied yourself for years.

   Use simple movements and expressions, ones you can repeat and easily perform. There is no right or wrong way of using this technique, but it should not be used to interfere with the free will of another.

7. Use a proper and appropriate choice of movements. If your dance is to bring love into your life, allow them to be smooth, sensual, and drawing. If it is a magickal pantomime for greater strength in a particular part of your life, the movements might be more regimented, stronger, and assured. Every movement should have a purpose, symbolic or otherwise.

8. Methodically prepare the scene and area for your magickal pantomime. Decide on the appropriate atmosphere and prepare the aids for it. Decide on the fragrance most reflective of the energy of your dance. Decide on appropriate candles, music, and costume for your magickal pantomime. Later in this chapter there are ideas for various costumes that you can create to further empower your dance. In the bibliography there are several sources on magickal aromatherapy, colors, and candles. The more consciously we choose these, the more power we add to the ritual.

9. Magickal words can be joined with the dance. They can be in the form of prayers, affirmations, poetry, or the use of god-names—all of which reflect the purpose and energy of your magickal dance. Insert them before, during, and/or after the actual movements to re-enforce and strengthen the focus.

10. Take at least a week to set up and prepare your magickal dance pantomime. By focusing and developing your dance over this period, it allows the subconscious to release increasingly more energy to be actualized through the ritual.

By taking a week to prepare, you build a thoughtform of positive energy that facilitates its manifestation and you will be able to work on the dance without excluding other responsibilities. It only takes 15 to 30 minutes a day to dance greater abundance, fulfillment, love, and joy into our lives. We dissipate our energies through so many things and so many people; we owe it to ourselves to spend at least this much time daily doing something creative for ourselves.

Over a period of time you will build up a catalogue of magickal dances you can draw on and employ as they are needed.

Once the magickal dance pantomime is prepared, the ritual procedure is followed as we have described previously. Begin by marking off your sacred space and then enter the circle. Perform the *Rending of the Veils* and allow the sacred space to fill with creative energy. Balance yourself with the appropriate movements, and then offer any prayer, poetry, or affirmations you have chosen for your magickal pantomime.

Begin your dance pantomime. Act out the purpose. See and feel yourself fulfilling it through the dance. Make it as real as possible. Know that as you perform these movements, energy is being set in motion so your purpose can be accomplished in the physical world. Know that new conditions and opportunities are going to be created for you. Become the energy, letting it fill you as you move. The energy will empower your life in accordance with the purpose of the dance.

After the magickal pantomime, assume one of the physical attitudes—sitting, kneeling, standing, or prostrate. Simply feel and experience this new energy pattern you have created for your life by this dance. Visualize yourself accomplishing everything you symbolized in your dance. Offer a prayer of thanksgiving, an affirmation, or some verbal acknowledgment.

Perform your balancing exercises again to stabilize this newly released energy within you. Take three steps back and perform the *Closing of the Veils*. Dissipate the sacred circle's energy, and leave the area with confidence in the dance's power of manifestation.

Group Dances

Group work in magickal dance requires more organization. In group work it is the group's energy and not the individual's that is the key to success. With groups, an intensified and expanded energy and experience will occur. There may be a central dance figure, but it is the group and its collective strength which will give the ritual dance its true power. With group dance, as with any group ritual, the dance is only as powerful as its weakest member.

Circle dances and spiraling motions lend themselves easily to group movements. The more linear the movements, the greater the power is raised. *Simplicity is a must!* Confusion in the movements will invoke confused and disruptive energy.

One of the simplest ways of choreographing group dance is to create a sacred space at the beginning and dissipate it at the end. Symmetry of steps is important and powerfully effective. As the ritual group enters, the first member begins to encircle the area. The circle should be large enough so each member of the group has room to move without walking on the heels of the person in front of them.

As the marking off begins, the first member should establish the rhythm of steps. An effective rhythm is two steps forward and one step back. With each rotation around, a new member of the group falls in behind, joining in the rhythm. This movement is very effective in altering consciousness, and can be used in some ways to induce trance. Forward, back. In, out. Heaven, earth.

As each person enters into the circle and joins the rhythm, the first person should fall in behind the last person to enter the circle. The number of rotations around the circle will vary. Use what is appropriate to the ritual's purpose or what is effective for your group. One way to determine the rotations is by the number in the group. If there are ten members, there should be at least ten rotations, each one drawing in a member. There should also be three rotations with the entire group in the circle to create group harmony and strength.

On the last rotation, the leader should be back at the original point. As the dancing stops, all members of the group should take one step forward in unison—a symbol of entering within the sacred space. This can be done on the word of the group leader. The leader can then indicate to the members to assume one of the four physical attitudes. The leader should remain standing.

The leader then enters further with the traditional three steps forward and *Rends the Veils*, opening the energies for everyone within the group. An affirmation, a statement of purpose, or an opening prayer is effective. At this point, the leader either performs the dance himself or herself or takes by hand a member from the circle to perform the dance.

A nice aspect of groups is that ideas and the choreographing can be done together, providing greater creative input. There are usually members within the group who are musically inclined and can provide some of the music themselves. More and more people are learning to drum in ritual form.

After the performance and the assimilation of the energy, the veils should be closed and the group should stand and take a step back to the outer edge of the sacred space. Then the dance movement is repeated, only in a counterclockwise direction. With each rotation around the circle, a member of the group exits the ring.

Again, keep the moves simple. Allow for participation by everyone. The actual magickal pantomime may fall to several individuals in particular, but everyone should participate in it at some point. Everyone should get a chance to lead the dance and establish its rhythm. Even though one or two members may be more skilled in dance, every member should get an opportunity to perform the actual magickal pantomime within the sacred space. Remember that it is not the skill, but the enthusiasm for the participation that will raise the most energy.

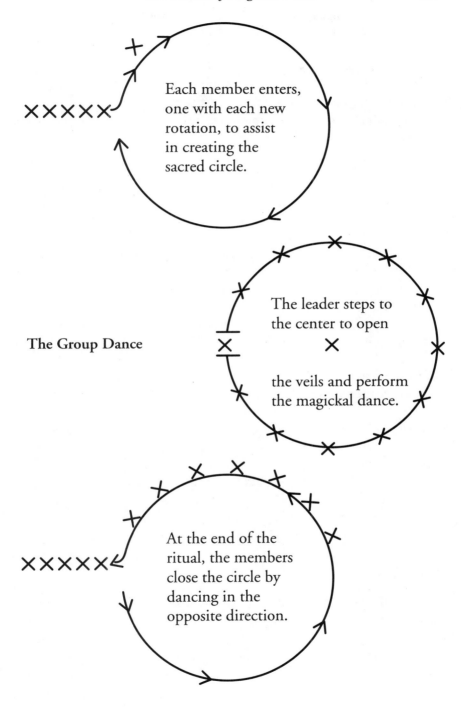

Each member enters, one with each new rotation, to assist in creating the sacred circle.

The Group Dance

The leader steps to the center to open

the veils and perform the magickal dance.

At the end of the ritual, the members close the circle by dancing in the opposite direction.

Decorating the Body for Magickal Dance

The body is often decorated in ritual to enhance its power and to help create altered states of consciousness. Body decorating can be simple or elaborate and can involve actual body art or various kinds of costuming. We will explore three simple ways of enhancing and empowering dance through ritual decorations:

Body Art

The body can be painted to enhance the significance of the dance. This assists in invoking the archetypal energies. Many societies employed this as part of their ritual. The face, hands and other parts of the body can be marked with signs, symbols, images and colors that reflect the purpose of the dance.

Tattooing is one of the most ancient forms of body art. I don't recommend it due to possible health complications and because of its permanence. An alternative would be body painting. There are many face-painting kits on the market today. These are hypo-allergenic and are easily washed off with soap and water. Thus, you can more easily adjust the body marking to the ritual.

In chapter ten, there are samples of magickal alphabets. Painting words, phrases, and images upon the body or even upon the costumes is a way of empowering yourself. You can even inscribe your own name in one of these magickal languages upon yourself. This helps to awaken the magickal essence within you during the dance.

Many individuals will take on magickal names that represent their spiritual and magickal quest in life. These can be painted upon the body and the ceremonial costumes as preparation for the magickal dance. It is fun, creative, and empowering.

Ceremonial Costumes

Robes and ceremonial dress for dance rituals should be simple and allow for freedom of movement. If there is a particular magickal tradition that you follow, your ceremonial costume can be made in the style of that tradition. On the following pages are some simple robe designs that allow for ease of movement.

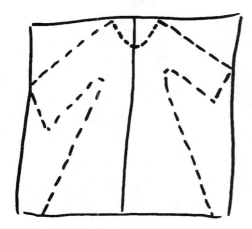

- Lay out your pattern.
- Cut out along the pattern and sew together.
- Decorate it personally.

Making Your Magickal Robe

The Himation or Toga   **The Stola**

Greek Traditional Robes

The style of robes depicted above are from the ancient Greek and Roman traditions. The Himation or Toga wrap was common menswear. It was loose and comfortable, allowing for freedom of movement. One arm was left bare with the ends tossed over the opposite shoulder. It was usually pinned to prevent falling. The female stola was a drape robe tied just below the breasts. It was allowed to drape and fold loosely down.

The Babylonian Tradition— used to imitate and dance to the gods and goddesses.

The Egyptian Tradition— the dancer's loincloth. The loincloth was often used in ritual dance by men and women for its ease of movement.

Other Sample Dance Robes

Making a meditation or ceremonial robe does not require great skill. If you have difficulty sewing, find someone to assist you. Fabric store personnel can be helpful, and most stores have patterns for robes.

One of the simplest ways to make a robe is to buy a large section from a bolt of cloth in a color you feel comfortable with. White, black, or gray are neutral and applicable to almost any ritual or dance. If you are part of a group, a particular color may be required.

Measure the length so it will be proper for you and fold the cloth so that the ends meet in the middle, and then mark off a pattern similar to the one depicted in the illustration. Then simply cut along that pattern and sew along the sides and the sleeves.

Take your time with this. As you work on it, realize that this robe is going to become magnetized with the creative energy of every ritual and meditation that you do. Use it as a tool of energy.

Once sewn, you can sash it at the waist with a cord. The cord should be long enough to wrap around you three times. Three is the creative number, the number of new birth. And it is new birth that we will achieve through our dances and our other magickal meditations.

Decorate it with signs and symbols that are important for you. If there is a particular tradition you are drawn to, use symbols and images from it. If there are specific qualities you hope to unfold in the course of your rituals, use them. These can be painted on. Most fabric stores offer paints that can be put on cloth permanently. Be creative. Have fun. Make your robe unique.

Ceremonial Masks

Traditionally masks were made to frighten away natural enemies, to resist evil spirits, for protection, for success, and for fertility. In ritual, they can be used for almost any purpose. The masks can be worn or they can be used to decorate the temple area as well.

Masks help us to enter into the imaginative world. They help create illusions. They facilitate connecting with the supernatural. They help suppress one personality while encouraging the assumption of another. Masks are a dynamic tool for shapeshifting, bringing out the persona and energy associated with the mask—be it a deity or warrior.

A Stick Mask

A Domino Mask

An Eagle's Head Hat Mask

A Helmet Mask—
The Iroquois Twisted Face

Types of Masks

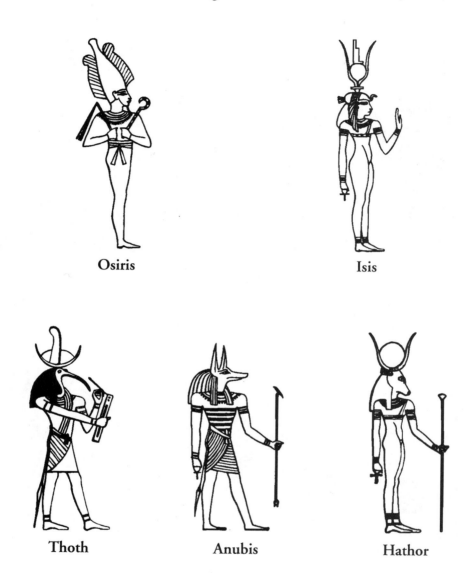

Osiris

Isis

Thoth

Anubis

Hathor

Egyptian Headdresses

Hat masks based on the head pieces of the Egyptian gods and goddesses are effective to use in dance ritual to attune to them.

There are many types of masks. The most popular is the domino mask which was first used in 16th century Italy. They cover the upper half of the face—some as far as the lips and some only as far as the nose. There are also full helmet masks which cover the head and face, often resting on the shoulders. If you prefer to have your face uncovered, use a hat mask which rest atop the head and generally leaves the face uncovered. Lastly, there is the stick mask, which is difficult to employ because it doesn't leave both hands free.

Ritual is a creative process. So too, is the making of costumes and imbuing them with energy. Making a mask is fun, but for the mask to be effective it must be secure and comfortable and should not restrict breathing, speech, or sight. The last section of this chapter provides directions on making a mask. It is a foundation upon which you can build, decorate, and create.

Making a Ceremonial Bird Mask

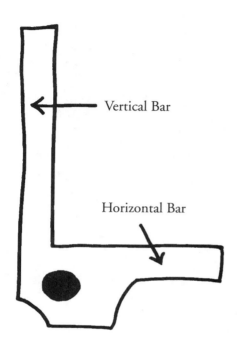

Vertical Bar

Horizontal Bar

The Basic Shape

1. Take a large piece of paper and fold it in half.

2. The paper must be large enough so the vertical bar shown in the diagram will go over the top of the head.

    The horizontal bar must be long enough to go around the head and overlap at the back.

3. When the horizontal and vertical flaps are fastened, the mask will fit over your head like a hat.

4. Adjust the fit so the mask will rest comfortably on the bridge of the nose.

5. This basic shape is the foundation upon which you can make a wide variety of mask images—animal and human.

6. Take a second piece of paper and fold it in half. Sketch the pattern as shown in the illustration.

   The more curve you put in the bottom part of the drawing, the more curve the beak will have.

   Experiment, square and rectangular shapes can be used for animal muzzles.

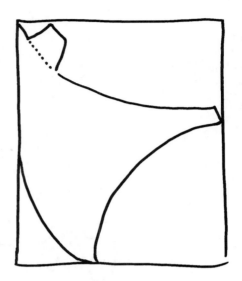

7. Now cut along the lines and fasten it onto the basic shape from described in step five. The small flaps at the top can be fastened to the outside of the basic shape, or you can cut two slits into the basic shape and feed them through. They can be glued or fastened on the inside and won't show.

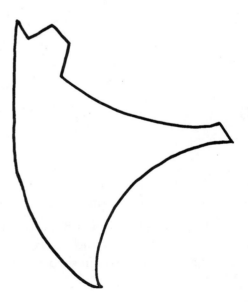

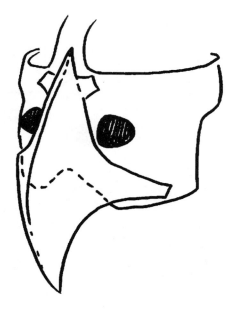

8. At this point, you can paint, color, and further decorate your
   mask. Attach streamers and feathers.

   Use colors that will be appropriate for your purpose. Be creative.
   See yourself as a creative, magickal being bringing to life a tool
   that will assist you in shapeshifting when you dance.

Adding Power to Dance Through Masks

Body Painting and Decorating for Magickal Purposes

Part Two

Sacred Dances of Power

CHAPTER SEVEN

SPINNING WHEELS AND CIRCLE DANCES

The circle is an old and universal symbol, having power and motion in both the physical and spiritual realms. It is the archetypal symbol for wholeness. The circle symbolizes the wheel of life that turns constantly and reflects perpetual movement in our lives. It has no beginning and no end, reminding us that we can start our own unique dance of life at any point and become creative.

The circle represents all that is not manifest, along with all that is possible. It symbolizes the womb, primal feminine energies, illumination, intuition, and creative imagination. But for them to benefit our lives they must be brought forth, out of the circle into the womb of physical expression. The divine feminine, in its symbol of the circle, becomes the gate through which we may enter or leave life's mysteries.

The circle has an inner and an outer aspect. The outer is our life activities. The inner is the power of creativity that we can draw on to shapeshift the outer reality. The outer aspect is the masculine and the inner aspect is the feminine. When we merge the two through dance, innate creative energy is released and new birth occurs.

The circle is a symbol for the sun. The sun revolves around the heavens and represents wholeness that comes from balancing opposites. In the physical world, we draw life from the sun.

123

Life's energies are cyclical. This is why it also has ties to the moon and subtle inner energies affecting our lives. The lunar phases reflect subtle energy changes. The moon also has a light and a dark side, indicating inner and outer expression.

The circle teaches us that we cannot separate who we are—our inner circle, from what we do—our outer circle. It is a guide to discovering our spiritual essence and how best to manifest it within the circumstances of our lives.

This is reflected in the circle dance. Sacred circle dances are very ancient. The more ancient dances were repetitious, involving continuous circling. This repetitive circling reminds us that if our life lessons are not learned, we are destined to repeat them again and again. When we merge our outer circumstance with higher inner awareness, the lesson is learned, and we spiral up into a new circle of life.

The circle dance is a sacred drama, employing physical action to alter mind and consciousness. It is a means to awaken deeper consciousness through physically enforced concentration. Through the physical circling, the individual spirals to new levels of perception.

The dancing of the circle symbolizes the sun and the moon—the male and the female together. When the sun and the moon—the inner and the outer—are joined, the dance of life begins.

Circle dancing is a sexual act because it the releases creative energy, creating wholeness. We are all a combination of male and female energies. Often they are out of balance. The circle dance creates a place of sacredness—a point where there is no separation of male and female, night and day, darkness and light, positive and negative, physical and spiritual.

The center of the circle is a focal point, the bindu. All dance, particularly circle dance, is a series of rhythmic steps around a central point. That central point can be an altar, a fire, an individual, an idea, or a prayer. The dancing adds energy to that point within the circle. Dancing around the bindu creates a vortex of energy. This vortex helps seal out extraneous energies, while protecting and empowering the bindu for manifestation.

There is often a question regarding which direction to dance the circles, clockwise or counterclockwise. Either way, a spiral of energy called a columnar wave in modern physics is released. Different direc-

The Ouroboros

The Ouroboros is a symbol for eternity and the continuity of time. When we dance a magick circle, we awaken the Great Serpent of Life. We link the inner and outer realms through the force of our primal creative energies.

A powerful way of activating this force is dancing in a circle with a rhythm of two steps forward and one step back. Visualize a great serpent of force and life beginning to take form within the perimeter of the dance. This great serpent not only separates the inner and the outer worlds, but joins them as well. Step within the circle and renew your life force.

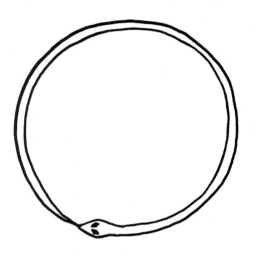

The Bindu

The bindu is the focal point in the circle dance. It is the prayer, the affirmation, the purpose, the hope, wish, or dream that the energy of the dance will be directed to manifestation.

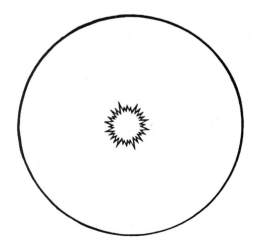

tions result in different effects from the columnar wave that is created.

Clockwise or deosil movement is the activating of the energy, that is considered more masculine, more outwardly energizing. It has a centrifugal effect, pulling energy out from the inner realm. It draws the spiritual out into the physical world. It charges, strengthens, and stimulates power. In healing circle dances, it energizes the aura and strengthens the overall balancing process. It evokes energy from the inner realms so they can manifest more fully in the physical realms.

The counterclockwise or widdershins movement is inward or receptive energy. The spiral created is drawing in. It takes you from outer to inner consciousness, facilitating going within oneself. This movement can be effective in exploring time and past life connections. It stimulates the feminine energies of intuition, illumination, and creative imagination. It awakens a greater sense of timelessness and opens the power of the past, present, and the future that live within you. It is a grounding and balancing movement.

When the two movements are employed together within the dance, the waves of energy intertwine. A helix type of spiral is formed around the bindu—the focus of the dance. This results in an energy for manifestation of the bindu.

The dancing raises the kundalini energy or the creative life force. Spirals are raised up like the ancient serpent of power. This activates, healing, wisdom, new realization, and new birth. It is the awakening of the pure creative life force!

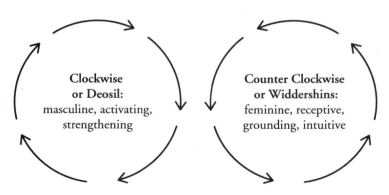

Importance of the Dance Direction

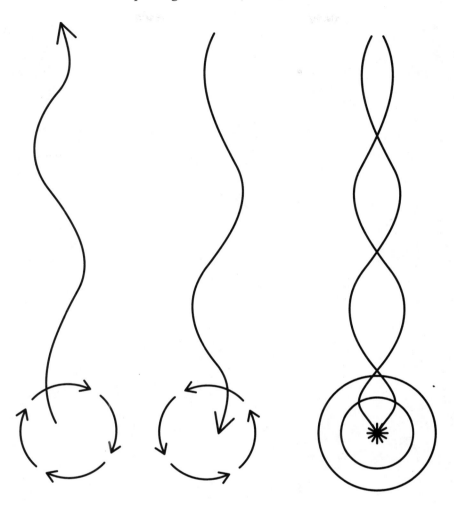

Energy Waves Created Through Movement

Clockwise	Counter Clockwise	Both
Draws energy out from within. It is both masculine and centrifugal.	Draws energy in from the outside. It is feminine, receptive, and grounding.	When both directions are used in dance, a helix type of vortex is created around the bindu. Male and female forces unite to give birth to a focal point. Manifestation begins!

Raising the Creative Life Force Through Dance

A Magickal Prayer Dance

There is a very simple way of dancing our prayers into manifestation. For this, you will need at least two other people. It is better if the other two participants are male and female, but it is not essential.

This dance draws its power from both directions being danced simultaneously, creating a vortex around the individual in the bindu of the circle. These movements will activate the corresponding masculine and feminine energies.

1. Begin by marking off the sacred space, encircling the area at least three times in a clockwise direction.

2. Whoever's prayers are to be danced into manifestation will serve as leader and step within the circle and *Rend the Veils*. The other two members should be on opposite sides of the circle.

3. Perform the balancing exercise, and speak the affirmation or prayer you wish to empower. Then sit and as you do, the other two participants will begin to encircle the area, one dancing clockwise and the other dancing counterclockwise. A rhythm of two steps forward and one step back is effective. While they dance, you meditate on the manifestation of your prayer.

4. To further empower the movements, have the participant that dances clockwise raise up and down on his or her toes while dancing the circles. The up and down movement activates masculine energies. If the individual finds this difficult, he or she can bob the upper body forward and back which also further activates masculine energy.

   The participant dancing counter-clockwise to activate the feminine energy should incorporate a side-to-side movement to amplify the energy. Swaying and swinging the hips will also activate the feminine energy.

5. While these circles are being danced, the individual in the middle visualizes and meditates on the fulfillment of the prayer. See it coming to life for you. From the moment you close the circle, the process is set in motion in the physical realm.

6. When you know you have fulfilled your purpose, stand. The other dancers should recognize this as a clue. They should complete the circle they are now dancing and then stop, on opposite sides of the circle, just as when they began.

7. Perform the balancing movements. Offer any prayer or affirmation of thanksgiving. Take three steps back from the center and perform the Closing of the Veils. As a group, close the ritual and bring the energies into manifestation by encircling the area three times in a counterclockwise direction.

Magickal Spiral Dance

Spiralling and spinning motions are powerful ways of using circular movements. They create a powerful vortex of energy that speeds up the activities of our own energy centers, called chakras.

Chakras mediate all energy going into and out of the physical body, and though not part of the physical body, chakras are intimately connected to it. For us to be able to access higher, subtle energies and bring them into our physical consciousness, these centers must operate more fully. This can be accomplished by dancing spiral and spinning dances.

Spiral Dances

The spiral symbolizes the evolution of the universe and anything within it. It is associated with both the creative and the destructive forces of the universe. The clockwise spiral is the creative and releasing motion. The counter-clockwise spiral is the destructive and forming motion.

Dancing Your Prayers into Manifestation

An up and down motion, such as raising and lowering on your toes, while dancing clockwise, will amplify the masculine energies. If you prefer, a bobbing motion can be employed. This motion also stimulates the masculine energies. Both movements are symbolic of the assertive masculine forces.

Dancing Your Prayers into Manifestation

The participant who dances counter-clockwise should incorporate side to side movements. These can be a swinging of the hips or just a swaying motion side to side. The side to side sway is effective to do anytime that you need to relax and balance yourself. It calms and it is grounding, it also activates the intuitive faculties.

Life does not exist without both motions. We are constantly tearing down the old to build the new. We can't accomplish one without the other. It draws us into and out of the unmanifested forces of the universe.

Many of the ancient spiral dances were designed to stimulate fertility, to activate healing, and to induce ecstasy. Spiral dances can be done singly or in a group.

Group spirals are not only beautiful if kept simple, but they are powerful, affecting the most intimate energies of the participants. The diagram will suggest different ways of working with them.

One of the most effective dances is to spiral from the outer perimeter of the temple circle to an inner circle. Of course, the availability of space will determine just how much spiraling can be done.

Songs and chants, recited in unison, tremendously empower the spiralling motion. Such songs and chants should be kept simple. The chant while spiralling in using a counter-clockwise motion, can be an expression of what the group is seeking. As the spiral moves back out from the center in a clockwise motion, the chanting should affirm the reception or manifestation of the desired goal.

The group should see themselves caught in a great universal vortex that draws them into a central divine source of power from which each person draws whatever is most needed. Then the dance spirals out from that center to the circle of the outer perimeter.

Depending upon the size of the group and the purpose of the ritual, the spiralling in and spiralling out can be repeated several times. One way to determine the number of times to spiral is through basic numerology, in accordance with the purpose.

Always make sure you have a definite beginning and an end to the dance for before and after the spiralling. This stabilizes the energy of the group which can become very intense. This repetitious spiralling induces strong altered states. It can become hypnotic when used with chanting. Grounding and balancing are essential.

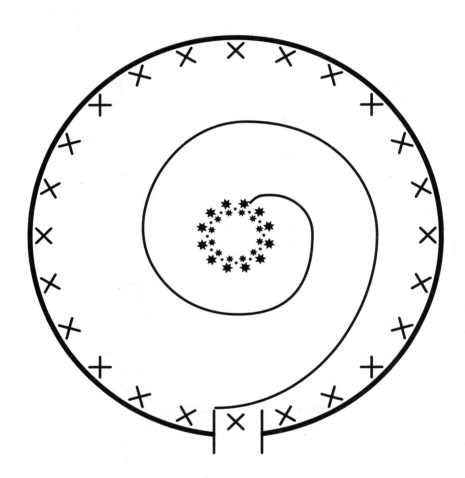

The Spiral Dance

 As you spiral into that which is not manifest, you touch and activate the primal energies within yourself. As you spiral out, you draw those energies out with you so they can manifest themselves and bless your physical life.

Spinning Dances

Spinning is symbolic of bringing forth life. It is the fostering of new growth. There are many tales and myths of how life was spun into existence. Spider tales reflect the aspect of spinning new creations.

Dances that employ whirling and spinning are very powerful. Whirling initiates dynamic energy that can sometimes be difficult to balance. For those just beginning, I recommend that spinning and whirling be done in a clockwise direction, and if it is to be done counter-clockwise, do only as many counter-clockwise revolutions as were done clockwise.

Whirling stimulates our whole energy system. It induces a strong altered state of consciousness. It loosens the etheric webs of our subtle energy field so that the energy flowing into and out of the physical body is stronger and more vitalizing.

Whirling can be taken to extremes, as is done by some of the whirling dervishes. These kinds of extremes are detrimental. The chakras are overstimulated and release an unbalanced amount of psychic energy which is difficult to harmonize.

Whirling can be performed in magickal dance to elicit easier access to levels of consciousness and energy that are not normally so accessible. It is most effective when incorporated as part of the whole ritual and not used only by itself.

Create and mark off your sacred space, as you have learned. Enter in and open the veils. Balance the energy. And then use the whirling in some of the manners listed later in this section. These are only guidelines. At the end, balance, close the veils, and dissipate the sacred circle as always.

Whirling is a wonderful way of helping manifest your magickal body or image. As you whirl, visualize yourself being transformed within its energies, so that as you complete your revolutions you are your most magickal, ideal self. This can be a prelude to other specific dance purposes. It will empower the bindu.

How many rotations should you do? There are a number of ways of determining the number of rotations you should perform. What is most important, though, is that the number of rotations should have significance for you and your dance ritual.

Use a number of rotations that is equal to your Life Path number in numerology. This is the single digit number that is based on your birthday. To do this, reduce your birth date to numbers and add them all together. The month number is determined by how it falls in the year. For example, June is the sixth month and so its number is 6.

Example: April 27, 1958 = 4+2+7+1+9+5+8 = 36 = 3+6 = 9

When the total is achieved, reduce it by adding the individual digits until you get a number of ten or less, giving you the basic number of rotations. Each number has its own ability to awaken specific kinds of energies that are associated with it. Refer to the chart below.

WHIRLING ROTATION MAGICK

Number of Rotations	The Energies Activated
1 or 10	Strength of will; independence; originality; initiation
2 or 11	Rhythm of astral plane; dream consciousness; feminine energies; psychic realm
3	Energies of blessed souls; creativity; art and inspiration
4	Energies of devas; balance and harmony; laying new foundations
5	Awakening the microcosm; Mother Nature; freedom; versatility; psychic power
6	Feminine, mothering energies; healing; education; home and family
7	All energies of healing; self-awareness; truth; knowledge of old and new
8	Energies of the gods and goddesses; occult wisdom; balance and power
9	Healing empathy; transition; endings and beginnings; sensitivity

For the numbers one and two, use ten and eleven rotations to get the fullest effects. Experiment. Study numerology and work out your own significances. After performing the rotations sit and meditate within the sacred space, assimilating this new energy.

Creating a Vortex Through Magickal Spinning

While within your sacred space, spin something new into existence for yourself. See yourself drawing your wish, hope, or dream out and into manifestation. Practice, spinning certain colors into manifestation so that you can absorb and use their energies. Do not be afraid to experiment with this.

If dizziness occurs or becomes too strong during the creation of a vortex, stop immediately. With practice, the body will be able to handle the rotations without discomfort. You are simply helping your essence become acclimated to the new energy. Remember that to be a magickal dancer is to be a magician—an alchemist. The important factor is to know you are doing something physical to align with the ethereal energies you wish to manifest within your life.

As you experiment with spinning and whirling within your sacred dance you will find that the effects may not seem as strong as in the beginning. This does not mean you should increase the number of revolutions. It is simply a positive sign of growth, indicating that your energy has grown. You are developing the magickal ability to spin and weave your energy into new patterns!

Creating a Vortex Through Magickal Spinning

Stand erect with arms outstretched. Focus your attention on your purpose. See yourself within the sacred circle, standing between worlds. As you begin your spinning, do so at a speed that is comfortable for you. See and feel the energy swirling in and around you as if you are part of a great creative, spiritual tornado. See yourself changing into your magickal image and becoming empowered with this act. Know that what you set in motion is real.

Creating a Vortex Through Magickal Spinning

Linking with the Primal Feminine

A widdershins, or counter-clockwise whirling, activates the feminine receptive energies within you and within your dance circle. Wearing a dark costume in such dance will enhance the linking with the primal feminine womb of life energies.

CHAPTER EIGHT

DANCE PRAYERS TO
THE DIVINE

W hen we attach special significance to our movements, especially when delving into the universe to touch the divine, we
are praying. We are praying through bodily movement.

Prayer is said to be a state of heightened awareness and communication. Prayers can be simple or complicated, both forms can work
for us. How effective the prayer is depends upon the import and
power we imbue it with. When we pray through movement, we unite
all aspects of ourselves for the purpose of growth and enlightenment.

It is not the movement, but our belief in the movement that
empowers it. Imbuing physical movement with intention frees and
strengthens us. It awakens our bodies to the spiritual world, allowing
it to nurture the body. We use prayers and wishes everyday, usually
without effect. But, when dance our prayers with power, we empower
our lives.

A powerful means of employing movement to align with a particular divine force is through the *Assumption of God-Forms*. This is
very similar to taking upon your own magickal image and body,
except that you assume the identity of a specific deity.

The gods and goddesses of all religions have been depicted in art and literature. Centered around these images is a powerful thought-form that has been created by all of the individuals who have worshiped and prayed to them. By creating a sacred space and aligning ourself with a deity through posture, pose, and costume, we invoke the energy associated with it. The priest or priestess of the dance becomes the god or goddess. Thus a priest or priestess working in the Egyptian tradition would assume the god-forms of Isis and Osiris through the magickal dance, becoming Isis and Osiris for the purpose of the dance.

These god-forms and the energy they represent within the universe are successfully invoked by an identification process. This is symbolized by a particular dress, movement, posture, and even prayers. The individual uses the external appearances connected with the god-form to stimulate the subconscious mind to align with its energies in the universe.

Assumption of the God-Form Through Dance

Assumption of god-forms is a powerful tool for enlightenment, but the participant must understand the symbolism of the movements and dress appropriately. If you are working within a particular magickal tradition, learn as much about that tradition as possible. Read myths and tales about gods and goddesses within the tradition.

Many of the ancient gods and goddesses had positive and negative aspects, and unless you are aware of these qualities, your magickal dance may stimulate more than you can handle. See the end of the chapter for list of the aspects of some god and goddesses to help you get started.

1. Begin as always by creating your sacred space. As you do so you may wish to see that space filling with a color that has come to be associated with the particular god or goddess.

2. Enter within and *Open the Veils.* As you do, see this influx of energy swirling around and filling you. Imagine yourself being

Assumption of the God-Form

Through the magickal dance—by identification through costume, posture, gesture, and movement—the priest and priestess become the god and goddess. If the individuals are working in the Egyptian tradition, their dance would create a sacred space where they could assume the god-form energy of Isis and Osiris. Through the magickal dance, they become Isis and Osiris to fulfill the dance's purpose.

transformed, becoming the god or goddess. If you are not wearing a costume symbolic of the deity, put it on at this time.

3. Balance yourself and assume a meditative position. Take time to reflect upon the symbolism and powers associated with the deity. If there are specific poses and gestures associated with this deity, slowly and deliberately perform them at this time. Imagine and feel yourself becoming one with the deity.

4. If you are unsure of the various movements, gestures, and postures of a particular deity, examine art and literature of the particular tradition. Many of the gods and goddesses are depicted in very symbolic poses; these will help you to assume the godform.

5. To help you empower yourself once in the sacred space, you may wish to have learned something about the folk dances of that area of the world.

    Often the folk dances carry remnants of the religious significance of more ancient dances. It also helps you to understand how the people move, for people dance differently in different parts of the world. In some areas the head may be the center of expression, while in others the hands and arms are. It will vary from country to country.

6. Take time near the end to see yourself absorbing the energy of the deity. See this energy as being born within you, an energy that you will take out with you from the circle to empower your daily life.

7. Rebalance yourself, close the veils, and then dissipate the sacred circle.

One of the most common questions that arises in the assumption of god-forms is whether or not a male individual can assume the god-form of a female and a female assume the god-form of a male. The answer is *Yes,* but it is more difficult. A female will more easily resonate and be able to take on the form of a female deity than a male and vice versa.

The magickal dancer takes on in the course of the dance the magickal image representing the divine force he or she wishes to invoke.

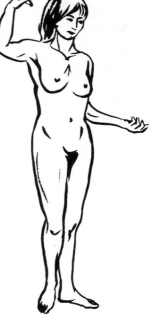

Through costume, masks, and movement the participant is able to set aside his or her own personality to align with the divine personality desired.

Invoking the Divine Force

This does not mean that the female god-form cannot be taken on by a male participant. It is just usually more difficult. This is one of the benefits of magickal dance. Using movements, postures, and gestures associated with the deity helps simulate the changes in the body and mind necessary to shift to that new consciousness.

We also must remember that, although the gods and goddesses are usually depicted as male and female, they are divine forces which are actually more androgenous—neither truly male nor female. They are beings who assumed a form that was most representative of the universal force and power they possessed. Along this same line, we are all a combination of male and female energies. Because of this, we can develop resonance with male and female deities. The deciding factors are the purpose of the dance and our own personal desire to attune and resonate with the deity. Our own sex does not exclude us from invoking and assuming any divine force.

The Mythical Traditions

Each mythology had its own tradition of rituals, music, and dance. Each tradition had its own means of awakening its members to the divine forces of that society. Each society had its own pantheon of gods and goddesses, symbolic of the universal forces and reflecting certain premises of that society.

What follows are some guidelines to forms that can be employed in magickal dance, based on four ancient magickal traditions; Greek, Egyptian, Celtic, and Teutonic. You are by no means limited to these four. They are examples to use as a starting point. Use the mythology to which you have always been attracted. Read the myths and tales associated with that tradition. Study about the customs and costumes of the society. They will assist in attuning and invoking the energies when used in the dance ritual.

As you read the myths and tales associated with the goddess or god you wish to invoke, you may find that they involve energies completely foreign to anything you have encountered in the physical world. This may indicate a need for greater harmony and balancing at the beginning and end of your magickal dance.

Male and Female Assumptions of God-Form

Our sex does not exclude us from invoking or assuming the godform of any deity. The purpose of the dance ritual and our personal desire to resonate with that divine force are the primary factors.

The Great Mother of the Bantu people of Africa is a being called Songi.

Assumption of her form awakens an energy of nurturing, love and great protection. Her energy brings the gifts of great wisdom, strength, compassion and fulfillment.

Most of the ancient gods and goddesses were fallible. They may have expressed and represented very divine characteristics, but many had human qualities as well. By assuming their form through dance, you open yourself to their strengths, as well as any weaknesses.

Choose the god or goddess according to your personal goals and not according to which one seems the most powerful. Complete resonance and assumption of the form with a lesser god or goddess can do more for you than a partial alignment with a major god or goddess. Use their symbols and colors to help the attunement.

Stay within a single tradition, rather than jumping around. Don't start one week with the Greek tradition and then move to the Celtic. Start with the one that attracts you the most. Work with it for an extended period first in study, then in meditation, and finally in dance. At least a year should be given to developing a working resonance. Learn to invoke its energies effectively before working with another system. Changing too often and jumping around creates discordant energies and it is unbalancing.

Most of the gods and goddesses had working relationships with others of their pantheon. Learning how they related to each other will help you to understand the energy that is invoked into your life through assumption of the god-form in magickal dance.

Many myths are tales of great beings who may have actually walked upon the earth, serving as teachers and helpers to humanity. Do not confuse the mythical with the unreal. The tales may be a blend of both.

There is often more going on within the myths than is apparent. There is usually more going on within our lives than what appears on the surface. Magickal dance with these mythical images will uncover this. When you align yourself with a deity of a particular mythology, you may activate events within your own life circumstances that are similar to those of the deity.

The Greek Tradition

This is the mythology of individuality, of becoming the hero or heroine of your life. The gods and goddesses work intimately with humans, providing weapons and tools necessary to accomplish the task at hand. As long as respect is paid, the individual will have awakened the powers to overcome hindrances.

The Orphic style of Greek ritual is filled with joy, music, song, and food. It was designed to develop a closeness with nature and with others. They are powerful dances when performed outdoors, clothed or unclothed. Others such as the Eleusinian dances were more formal.

GREEK GODS AND GODDESSES

Zeus . . . . God of thunder, air, and sky
Color: purple
Symbols: oak tree and eagle

Hera . . . . Goddess of marriage and all feminine energies
Color: emerald green
Symbols: scepter, cuckoo and peacock

Athena . . . . Warrior goddess of wisdom
Color: red-gold
Symbols: owl, helmet, aegis, shield, and spear

Apollo . . . . God of sun, prophecy, music, and art
Color: yellow-gold
Symbols: sun, archery, and lyre

Artemis . . . . Goddess of forest and moon
Color: amethyst
Symbols: bear and dog

Hermes . . . . God of communication, initiation, and magic
Color: silver
Symbols: caduceus, winged hat, and sandals

Ares . . . . God of war, strength, and passion
Color: scarlet
Symbols: all weaponry

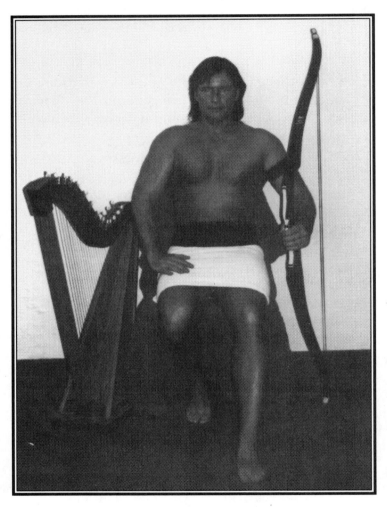

Assumption of the God-Form

Costume, posture, and props can be used to align oneself more easily with the archetypal energies represented by a mythological god or goddess. In this photograph, I am aligning myself with the energy of Apollo, the Greek god of prophecy music and art.

Assumption of the God-Form

Costume symbolic of and suitable for invoking the energy of the Greek god Pan can be easily used in dance to stimulate great joy and healing, as well as attunement to any of the four elements of nature. Pan dances are most effective when performed outdoors and to flute music of any kind.

Aphrodite . . . . Goddess of love and beauty
Color: turquoise
Symbols: dove, porpoise, girdle, and rose

Demeter. . . . . The mother goddess
Colors: brown and yellow
Symbols: cornflower and corn

Hecate . . . . Goddess of the moon, magic, and psychism
Colors: black with silver flecks
Symbols: black hooded cloak,
dark of the moon, hellhound

Persephone . . . . Goddess of new life, growth, and creativity
Colors: citrines, russets, and olive greens
Symbols: corn and pomegranate

Pan . . . . God of prophecy, nature, and healing
Colors: greens of the forest
Symbols: Pan flute, ivy, songs, and pine cone

Other gods and goddesses are easily adapted to magickal dance in this tradition. Dionysus, the god of magic and healing, was the source of much inspiration and ceremonial dance. Even Hades, the god of the underworld, can be invoked through dance, although he is less likely to express himself in front of others. A study of the myths and the major personas will elicit much dance inspiration.

The Egyptian Tradition

The Egyptian tradition is more formal in its ritual. It had effects upon almost every major society as a center of the mysteries. It is a tradition of alchemy, and the process of birth, death, and rebirth. Their ritual and dance often involved activating energies of mind over matter.

EGYPTIAN GODS AND GODDESSES

Ra . . . . God of the sun
Color: golden sunshine
Symbols: obelisk, hawk, and uraeus

Osiris . . . . God of wisdom, justice, and strength
Color: white and green
Symbols: tet (tree), crook, and flail

Isis . . . . Goddess of the moon and magic
Color: sky blue
Symbols: throne, wings, veil behind the throne,
a buckle

Horus . . . . Sun god of art, music, and healing
Colors: bright yellow and gold
Symbols: hawk and all-seeing eye

Bast . . . . Goddess of joy and animals
Colors: yellow gold and turquoise
Symbols: sistrum, the cat, and the lion

Thoth . . . . God of medicine, learning, and magic
Colors: violet and amethyst
Symbol: caduceus .

Hathor . . . . Mother god of protection
Color: coral
Symbols: mirror, sycamore tree, and cow

Nepthys . . . . Goddess of intuition and tranquility
Colors: pale greens and silver grays
Symbols: chalice and basket

Ptah . . . . God of craftsmanship and science
Color: violet
Symbol: mason tools

Anubis . . . . God of guardianship and guidance
Colors: black and silver
Symbols: jackal and sarcophagus

The Protective Gesture of Isis

The art and literature of the particular tradition can provide some wonderful clues to what movements and gestures might mean. Imagine and know that, as you perform movements and gestures within your sacred space you and the deity are one.

The Celtic Tradition

The Celtic tradition is one of romance, creativity and intuition. It is extremely adaptable and effective with magickal dance, especially outdoors around trees. It is primarily a matriarchal system and attuning to it tradition awakens inner intuition and creativity, allowing for very individualistic expression. The Celtic tradition helps you discover your inner fires and is rich in the magic of music, words, and dance.

Green is the predominant color. While forming the sacred circle during the dance ritual, visualize it filling with the rich, fertile green of Mother Earth. This will amplify any other dances, colors, and images used with this tradition. The assumption of the god-form in this tradition may reveal a color different than what is listed. Do not be surprised. When the energy manifests, it will often do so in a color whose energy resonates most closely to your own. Because of this, I have not provided a color for them.

CELTIC GODS AND GODDESSES

Dagda. . . . . The nourishing patriarch
Symbols: harp and cauldron

Danu . . . . Mother goddess of wisdom
Symbols: newly planted seed,
all symbols of water

Morrigan . . . . Goddess of magic and enchantment
Symbols: crossed spears and ravens

Cerridwen . . . . Goddess of magic and prophecy
Symbol: the great cauldron

Morgan Le Fay . . . . Fairy queen of magic and higher wisdom
Symbol: hand extending sword from the waters
of life

Brigid. . . . . Goddess of inspiration, healing, strength,
and endurance
Symbols: torches, fire, and well of
healing waters

Talieson . . . . God of prophecy, poetry, magic, and wisdom
Symbols: harp and staff

Rhiannon. . . . . Goddess of assertiveness, justice, and
the underworld
Symbols: gray horse and three sacred birds

Lugh. . . . . God of artistry, sun, and magic
Symbol: spear

Gwydion . . . . Guardian and guide
Symbols: images of science and law

The Teutonic and Norse Tradition

The Teutonic tradition is one of awesome power, beauty, magic, and violence. The energy of this tradition teaches great personal responsibility and the transmutation of energies. It is the tradition of learning to draw upon the force of our own inner magic and light.

The Teutonic tradition is rich in the magickal use of song and rhyme. Scaldcraft was the Teutonic method of using names, words, and poetry for magickal purposes. It was used to control one's own destiny and the destiny of others. The runes, the alphabet of this tradition, and the rhythm of the poetry were sources of power. In the next chapter, I provide postures based upon the vowels from the English alphabet. There are postures based on the runes as well, designed to physically activate the magic they symbolize. For further information on these runic postures, read *Futhark—A Handbook of Rune Magic* by Edred Thorsson.

TEUTONIC AND NORSE GODS AND GODDESSES

Odinor. . . . . God of knowledge, runes, poetry, and seership
Color: deep blue and indigo
Symbols: ravens and wolves, spear, and eight
legged steed

Frigga . . . . Goddess of abundance, weather, and herbal healing
Colors: deep greens
Symbols: golden spindle and necklace

Thor . . . . Warrior god of thunder and lightning
Colors: bright reds
Symbols: hammer, magic belt, and cart drawn by goats

Freyr . . . . God of plenty
Color: bright golden yellow
Symbols: bright sword, ship, and golden boar

Freyja . . . . Goddess of love, beauty, and prophecy
Color: soft reds and pinks
Symbols: falcon wings and a chariot drawn by cats

Balder . . . . Shining god of purity, healing, and mercy
Color: shining white
Symbol: all flowers, especially the balderblum

Tyr . . . . Bravest god and god of great strength
Color: dark red
Symbol: sacrificed hand

Heimdall . . . . Watchman god of the rainbow bridge
Colors: the rainbow
Symbol: the trumpethorn

Idun . . . . Goddess of beauty, rejuvenation, and youth
Color: gold and pastel blues
Symbol: golden apples

Bragi . . . . God of poetry and scaldcraft
Color: rich sky blue and sparkled with gold
Symbols: all songs, poetry, and musical instruments

CHAPTER NINE

AWAKENING THE ARCHETYPES

Understanding and working with symbology is essential to performing magickal dance. Symbology is the language of the unconscious. We employ ritual movement and dance to try to awaken and use its power.

To understand symbols is to understand ourselves, including our deep-rooted, instinctive capabilities. Symbology in dance helps open levels of our being that we have either been unaware of or ignored. Symbolic dance forms the bridge that enables us to cross from the mundane and rational to the primal and intuitive.

Learning to view all movement and aspects of life as symbolic is a means of awakening to the archetypal forces within life. An archetype is a primordial energy that is reflected by and works through the various elements in our life. We see the archetypal forces through the symbols of everyday life. These symbols reflect the power of the archetype and remind us of the universal power inherent in it. This is comparable to the manner in which the moon reflects the sun's light. The moon it is not a source of light, but because it reflects light, we are able to see more clearly at night.

Archetypal energies are universal. They are shared by all people and play within everyone's life in some manner. Carl Jung referred to them as part of the collective unconscious. They are the source of all energies experienced within physical life. In magickal dance, we use traditional symbols, images, and energies to manifest archetypes.

When we attach and use symbolic movement, we are reflecting into our lives the light of an archetypal force. The movements and postures lead us back to that source of light, helping us to merge the finite with the infinite within our present circumstances.

Many archetypal forces and patterns of those forces are definable. Thus with proper costume, movement, posture and gesture, those forces can be invoked into stronger play within our life. Working with and applying symbology of costume and movement to dance ritual will release the archetypal force. Such use of symbology focuses the attention and stimulates levels of the subconscious mind which is sensitive to and aware of the archetypal forces within our life.

There are even myths and tales that reflect specific archetypal energies. These tales and myths can be converted to ritual dance pantomimes. Role playing and dancing those tales within the sacred space is a consciously controlled means of awakening the archetypal energy and releasing it into your life. Simply follow the steps of magickal pantomime as given in chapter six.

The Archetypes Reflected Through Tales

Archetype of the Self

French tale *Master and the Pupil*
German tales *Tyll Ulenspiegel*
Italian tale *Jump into my Sack*
Egyptian tale *Promises of Three Sisters*
Pinocchio
Irish tale *Man Who Had No Stories*
South African tale *Mbega Kigego*

Archetype of the Feminine

All tales of the Goddesses
Snow White and Rose Red
Native American tale *How Men and Women Got Together*
Merlin and Nimue
Grimm's *Old Woman in the Forest*
Egyptian tale *Promises of Three Sisters*

Archetype of the Masculine	All tales of the gods
	Tales of Odysseus
	German tale *Master Thief*
	Native American tale *How Men and Women Got Together*
	Merlin and Nimue
	Labors of Hercules

Archetype of the Hero	Tales of Odysseus
	Atalanta and the Calydon Boar
	Rumpelstiltskin
	German tale of *Master Thief*
	Grimm's tale *Boy Who Went Forth to Find What Fear Was*
	Jason and the Argonauts

Archetype of the Adversary	Refer to last section of this chapter
	David and Goliath
	Jonah and the Whale
	German tale *The Goose Girl*
	Cinderella
	Snow White and the Seven Dwarves
	African tale *Old Crone and Iblees the Devil*

Archetype of Death and Rebirth	*Rumpelstiltskin*
	German tale *The Goose Girl*
	Dickens' *Christmas Carol*
	Crucifixion and Resurrection of Jesus
	Sleeping Beauty
	The Sword in the Stone
	African Bushman tale *Moon and the Hare*

Archetype of the Journey	Tales of Odysseus
	Grimm's tale *Boy Who Went Forth to Find What Fear Was*
	Biblical tale of Joseph and the Coat of Many Colors
	Alice's Adventures in Wonderland

The Seven Basic Archetypes

There are many archetypal forces operating in the world. There are astrological archetypes and there are archetypes of nature. Archetypes are reflected in every aspect of life.

Carl Jung broke the archetypal energies down into seven basic types, each reflecting specific kinds of energies operating within our lives. These seven types of energy manifest and reflect themselves through a variety of symbols, images, and activities. Understanding them will assist us in using dance, movement, and posture to intensify or soften their manifestation in our lives.

The following are descriptions of these seven archetypal forces and the primary symbols associated with them. These symbols can be employed in magickal dance in the form of costume and adapted to movement to activate these energies more strongly. Some suggestions are provided for this, but it is important that you find your own unique expression of the archetype. In this way, the Archetype of the Self is always dynamic and adds power to all other invocations and manifestations of these universal forces and energies.

As with all of the other techniques, while you employ movement and costume reflecting the archetype within the sacred circle, keep your focus on what you wish to accomplish by its activation. Make sure you take time at the end of any archetypal movements or postures to assimilate the energies and visualize the archetype coming to life for you when you step from the sacred space.

Archetype of the Self

This is the energy of our true self. It lies behind and beyond all of our personas and delusions of everyday life. It is our own individual primal energy source and our energy matrix. The Archetype of the Self is the source of our ego, individuality, creative abilities, gifts, potentials, and the source of our innate power.

All dance can be used to awaken the archetype of the self. This is the energy of inspiration for awakening the higher self within us. Movements, postures, and costumes which activate this archetype more strongly should help us to see a higher vision of ourself and inspire us to move toward our highest potentials. Dances to the self are inner calls to work and growth.

Symbols reflecting this particular force are homes and houses, books, temples, eggs, seeds, lit candles, births, weddings, and gifts. These can be used to decorate the sacred space or your costume to enhance the effects of your movements.

Dance Suggestions for the Archetype of the Self

- Pantomime building a new house or clearing the old.

- Free dance and move with a candle that you light in the midst of the ritual, bringing new light to life for yourself.

- Pantomime a wedding to symbolize union with the ideal you.

- Pantomime a dance in which you receive gifts in a specific area.

- Dance yourself coming out of an egg into new life or as a seed sprouting into new growth.

Archetype of the Feminine

We are all a combination of feminine and masculine energies which are expressed in many ways—yin and yang, magnetic and electric, negative and positive, or receptive and assertive. The feminine energy in life creates relationships. It is the flow and beauty of life. Feminine energy is intuitive, receptive, and accepting. It can nurture or it can suffocate.

The feminine reflects itself through mystery. It is the gate or doorway through which we enter or exit. It is the birth-giving energy, which is why movements of opening the veils and crossing thresholds are used in ceremonial dance. The feminine energy is the energy of illumination, intuition and creative imagination. Any imaginative or creative activity is an employment of the feminine.

There are many symbols of feminine energy—the cave, the womb, the vagina, breasts, fertility, night or darkness, thrones, the moon, tapestries, veils, water, beds, and spiders.

Dance Suggestions for the Archetype of the Feminine

- Dance with and through veils to new clarity. Stripping to pure nudity dynamically awakens the feminine energies.

- Perform the dance outdoors at night, under the light of the moon.

- Wear dark or black robes or dress to stimulate feminine energies.

- Pantomime a birth, coming forth from the great womb of life into new expressions of creativity.

Archetype of the Masculine

The archetypal masculine energies also exist within everyone without exception. They are the energies of fathering, assertiveness, making, directing, organizing, and building. The masculine archetypal is the aggressive, assertive, and penetrating energy of life. It initiates action and it urges us to action.

Our ability to assert the masculine helps us get the job done, just as our inability to assert it prevents the job from getting done. It is the energy of decisiveness and discrimination. It is the energy we need to activate when decisions need to be made. The masculine energy is impregnating energy; which initiates and opens new growth opportunities.

We can use movement and costume as a means of stimulating the masculine into greater activity. Some of the symbols for the masculine energy are the phallus, the sword, the sun, daytime, a tower, a scepter, and the male seed.

Dance Suggestions for the Archetype of the Masculine

- A dance with movements that are linear: straight, and forward.

- Pantomime crossing over and asserting yourself in new areas of life—crossing a line.

- Dances and rituals performed outdoors under the sun are very effective for regenerating the masculine energy.

- Pantomime a sowing of seeds or perform ritual plantings, such as trees. Whatever is planted should symbolize what you wish to initiate in your life.

Archetype of the Hero

Each and every one of us is the hero or protagonist in our lives. We must face difficulties singly and surmount them. In myths and legends, the hero conquers the foe and is victorious. In life, this does not always happen.

There may be obstacles in the work environment. There may be emotions that hinder our growth. Whatever must be faced and overcome is known as the *Archetype of the Adversary*. In part, we learn that things are supposed to go right. We are supposed to be victorious. We can use dance to awaken and facilitate this outcome within our own lives, to create opportunities to overcome our adversaries creatively.

The hero archetype provides insight into healing. If we find ourselves fighting and always struggling to surmount obstacles in life, we are being urged to draw upon the archetypal hero force more dynamically in our lives. Remember we are meant to win, although we may allow ourselves to be programmed to lose or be conquered.

Symbols of the hero archetype are images and scenes of battles, struggles, teachers, new knowledge, youth, shields, and healing balms.

Dance Suggestions for the Archetype of the Hero

- Pantomime battles in which you are victorious, using shields to protect yourself.

- Pantomime new knowledge and healing presented to you by a loving teacher or strong friend who eases your path.

Archetype of the Adversary

This force urges us to new strengths, new goals, and new discoveries of potential. The beasties and adversaries of life are all part of this archetype. This archetype helps us in finding new and creative ways of overcoming obstacles. Remember that every obstacle or hindrance can not be overcome through force or confrontation. It has been said that chaos forces creativity and such is the energy of this archetype.

Life is change. The Adversary is the agent of change in life which forces us to confront difficulties. The adversary destroys and wounds what is and manifests the unexpected. It tears down the old, so the new can rise in its place. It is the energy of fear, anger, and other strong emotions. It forces us to draw upon the creative forces of the hero archetype to achieve new success.

Much of the adversarial energy in our life is subtle. It is often the limitations we have imposed upon ourselves or allowed others to impose upon us. At some point in our growth we must break down those limitations.

To many, this energy is evil and many others will refrain from activating it through such a dynamic means as dance. We should invoke it at times, so we can see it in all of its guises. We can then confront it fully, with the brilliance of the soul.

We can create dances that involve the hero and the adversary together to facilitate an understanding of our obstacles and enemies while releasing energies to creatively overcome them. Dances to awaken the Hero archetype and the Adversary archetype are most effective when combined within a dance pantomime, like fighting an imaginary dragon. By learning to do this, we control the influence of adversarial energies in our life and facilitate the achievement of goals.

Determine before the dance what image best represents what you need to overcome. This can be a negative emotional attitude to a hindrance in your work environment. Choose an image that you can visualize easily. Then see yourself as the hero who will overcome it in a serious confrontation. The symbols of this archetype are all monsters, demons, and beasties. Suffering, tyrants, and walls needing to be scaled can also represent things that we wish to overcome.

Dance Suggestions for the Archetype of the Adversary

- Pantomime a ritual fight with an adversary or negative emotion.

- Assume positions, postures, and attitudes of a conquering hero.

- Play act climbing and struggling up a tall mountain to achieve a wonderful reward or prize.

- Take a negative habit and perform a ritual battle in which it is slain each morning within the sacred space until the habit disappears.

- Determine what you wish to tear down in your life so a process of rebuilding can occur. Dress as an adversarial being and pantomime the tearing down of the old.

Archetype of Death and Rebirth

All life is change. Everything is in a state of transition. At a certain point within our life, transition is more prominent. *The Archetype of Death and Rebirth* reveals the process of change. It stimulates the end of one aspect and the beginning of another. We die to be born and are born to die.

All change, all crisis, all sacrifice, all death, and all birth reflects this archetypal force in our life. If we can recognize the patterns of change, we can better handle them. We can also use ritual movement and dance to stimulate the process of change more actively. We can set energy in motion to manifest opportunities for death and rebirth in specific areas of our life.

All rites of passage and initiation ceremonies activate this archetypal energy. The sexual act can be performed ritually to free this energy along specific lines as well. Many tantric rites utilize this aspect. Some of the other symbols for this archetype are altars, clocks, all dances, scythes, crucifixions, and resurrections.

Dance Suggestions for the Archetype of Death and Rebirth

- Pantomime a death and a resurrection into new life.

- If you have an intimate partner, you may wish to perform the sexual act within the sacred circle to resurrect and empower the relationship.

- Pantomiming a physical death and resulting new life can be an effective way of overcoming an illness.

Archetype of the Journey

Our whole life is a journey of growth and evolution. Everything we encounter is part of that journey and affects its ease or difficulty. Just as the archetype of the Self is in every aspect of magickal dance, so is the archetype of the Journey. We are consciously using ritual movement to facilitate life movement.

Life is continual movement and development. This involves aging, building upon what has come before, opening to new directions, and opening to opposite directions. We are often unable to see

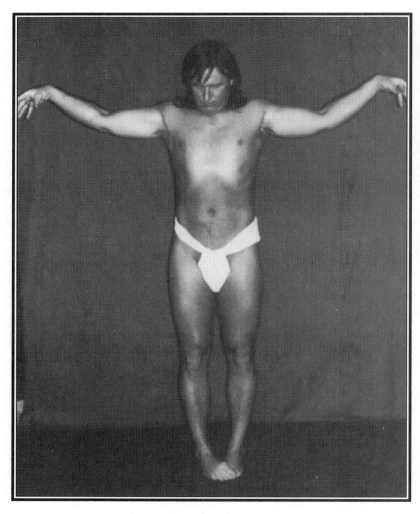

Dancing the Archetype of Death and Rebirth

Dancing the Archetype of Death and Rebirth

As we die to an aspect of one part of ourselves, we are reborn to another. Through magickal dance, we reach for new heights and new life expressions through that rebirth—as if we are coming forth from the womb.

our course in life. Sometimes, things may seem clear, and at others we may seem to be wandering aimlessly.

We can use dance and movement to stimulate information to clarify our present journey in life and to institute various course changes that can be more beneficial.

Some of the symbols of this archetype are trees, winding roads, labyrinths, climbs or ascents, traveling, rivers, pilgrimages, and staffs.

Dance Suggestions for the Archetype of the Journey

- Pantomime a journey through an area of your life of ups and downs, ins and outs, to an ultimate goal or reward.

- Pantomime moving through a labyrinth. You may wish to use a blindfold in part of it, then remove it midway through the dance. This symbolize the clarification your life's journey.

- Perform the *Tibetan Walk to Nowhere* from Part One.

All archetypal energies are neutral. At their highest and purest, they can only be experienced as positive, but as we go through the process of unfolding, they may reflect themselves positively or negatively within our lives. These seven archetypal energies have their own specific strengths, qualities, and applications through which we can identify them and utilize them through magickal dance.

As you learn to dance to awaken these archetypes, one will never be stimulated by itself. They all interact with each other, and aspects of several may actually manifest. They all dance with each other. As you dance with them, awakening them within the sacred space, their energies are released into manifestation in the outer world to change the dance steps of your outer life accordingly.

Dancing the Archetype of the Journey

The archetypal force of the journey is activated simply through postures and movements symbolic of the journey of life or our journey through one area of life. As we dance the archetypes, their energies are released into the outer life experiences, manifesting opportunities to apply them more creatively and productively.

CHAPTER TEN

CELESTIAL MOVEMENTS

In more ancient times, the people and students of the spiritual sciences were more aware of the influence of heavenly energies upon them. The imprints of the stars and the movements of the planets were a part of their life and their mind. One of the most powerful means of using magickal dance is in the re-imprinting energies of the stars upon the physical brain.

We can use physical movement and posture to imprint the movement and operations of the planets and stars upon our brain. We can use them to activate the play of their energies more dynamically within our lives.

The planets and the star constellations all reflect subtle forces that affect us. We can employ physical movements that mimic their movements and symbolize their energies. This invites them to play more intensely within our lives. At the same time, out of our own subconscious archives, we bring that ephemeral memory and attunement to the stars.

We can dance the glyphs for the stars and the planets. We can dance the constellation patterns as well. This heightens our awareness of them in our life, and enables us to become more sensitive to celestial movements and how they affect us personally. It heightens our awareness of how astrological configurations affect us through gravitational and other influences on physical, emotional mental, and spiritual levels.

By physically dancing the planets and constellations, we place ourselves within their rhythms, enabling them to work more creatively for us. Dancing the planets helps align our personal energies with the universal flow.

Dancing the planets opens a broad avenue for aligning the physical world with the celestial world. Ideally, we could learn to dance the entire astrological chart, enhancing the aspects that are most beneficial. This technique can be used to smooth over aspects of the chart which may be more difficult. The movements of the stars are intimately and subtly connected to our lives. Great strides can be made on many levels by anyone wishing to choreograph and dance the celestial movements.

The planets and the signs are symbols of specific forces and energies. Associated with them are glyphs, colors, fragrances, music, and movements which we can employ through magickal dance rituals. We will focus on the seven major planets and the twelve signs of the zodiac. These affect us most strongly. The outer planets of Neptune, Uranus, and Pluto also affect us, but not as often or as recognizably as the other seven. As you learn to work with the seven, you can then stretch yourself and create your own movements for the others.

Magickal Dance: Awakening the Powers of the Planets

Some of the correspondences are based upon Qabalistic teachings, but not entirely. The correspondences are also based upon experience using these movements, colors, and music to activate the energies most effectively.

Begin by determining which planet you wish to activate more strongly within your life. Read through the information presented in this section to assist you in understanding its forces. Also, read some beginning books on astrology to help you understand the energy and symbolism with the planet as well.

For each of the seven major planets, there is listed a general description of what can be attained by dancing their energies into activity. There will also be color and fragrances correspondences, music that is effective, and a magickal image that is associated with the planet. Assuming this image, rather than your own, will empower the entire dance ritual, manifesting its energies more effectively in your outer life.

I have also included a number for dance rotations. This number can be used to create the outer perimeter of the sacred circle and to use in spinning to take on the magickal image of the planet.

And lastly, I have included specific movements and postures to help you align physically with the heavenly body. Performing these while you visualize yourself in the magickal image will empower the whole exercise. After all of the correspondences are given, I will lead you through them, step by step, in a magickal dance.

The Sun

This dance will awaken a greater and higher sense of devotion, stimulates healing on all levels, activates opportunities for fame and success, harmonizes the body, stimulates inner vision of the beauty in all people and all things, and activates all the energies of the rainbow.

SYMBOL: ⊙   FRAGRANCE: Rose

COLOR: Yellow-gold   ROTATIONS: Six

MAGICKAL IMAGE: Child, Sacrificed God or Goddess, Majestic King

MUSIC: Handel's Messiah, Haydn's Creation, all sacred hymns

The Sun Salutation

This activates the inner sun. Massage the heart with right hand in circular motions. Place left hand over the heart and with the right hand lift energy from the heart to the head. Return right hand to rest on top of the left hand, over the heart area. Feel the inner sun shining throughout your body.

A. Circle your arms into prayer position at Christ Center.

B. Acknowledge the stars (suns) in the Heavens.

C. Bring the energy of the Sun to the Earth with the hands.

The Sun Salutation

D. Leg steps back;
head raises up, the
face is always
toward the sun.

E. Learn to let the
Sun support you
and give you
strength.

F. Our light—our
Sun—is humbled
before the Light of
Lights.

The Sun Salutation (continued)

G. We begin to rise—
like the cobra and
the Sun.

H. We lift ourselves
from the Earth.

I. We step forward
between the pillars
of the arms, and
face toward the sun.

The Sun Salutation (continued)

J. The Sun and Earth
    are together again,
    in you and through
    you.

K. Acknowledge the
    Sun and stars
    throughout the
    Universe.

L. Circle arms into
    prayer position at
    your own Sun
    Christ Center.

The Sun Salutation (continued)

The Moon

This dance awakens awareness of a divine plan in our life. It stimulates confidence, greater intuition and psychic ability. It can be used for emotional health and to stimulate dream activity and understanding of dreams. It opens perception of the tides of change within your life. It activates the feminine energies and helps us release our creative life force in a non-sexual way.

SYMBOL: ☽   FRAGRANCE: Wisteria

COLOR: Silver, violet   ROTATIONS: Nine

MAGICKAL IMAGE: Beautiful, strong naked man with silver slippers and a mirror.

MUSIC: Handel's Water Music; Chopin's Nocturne, or anything that evokes strong feelings

Moon Dance Movements

A. With these movements, we begin to free up the creative life force. Circle and half-circle the hips in crescent and full moon shapes. Let the hips swing free and full. Allow the hips to open wider and wider. This move deepens dreams and awakens psychic activity.

B. Place the dominant hand on the forehead and the other upon the sacrum. Push the head back and the hips forward slowly and deliberately. It is a posture of taking the released life force and using it to activate higher faculties.

C. This movement is a yoga position called the child's pose. It balances the creative life forces that are released. You are acknowledging the divine source of your own creative intuition. It stimulates a unique, independent expression of this creative life force.

Moon Dance Movements (continued)

Mercury

The dance for Mercury awakens awareness of the truth. It can be used to reveal falsehood or deception within our lives. It stimulates the ability to communicate and communication opportunities. It can be used to open up knowledge of magic and to stimulate opportunities for wheeling and dealing. It can be used to manifest educational endeavors and opportunities.

SYMBOL: ☿   **FRAGRANCE:** Rosemary

COLOR: Orange, yellow   **ROTATIONS:** Eight

MAGICKAL IMAGE: Hermaphrodite with caduceus wand

MUSIC: Mozart's Magic Flute, all woodwinds, flutes, horns

Mercury Dance Movements

A. Knowledge lifts us up, and the serpent of knowledge is a symbol for Mercury, thus the cobra posture is also used just as we learned earlier in this book.

B. With a slow, deliberate movement, imitate a serpent to bring yourself to a standing position.

Rise up and down on the toes, winding like a serpent.

Mercury Dance Movements (continued)

Venus

The dance movements for Venus are slow, expressive and seductive. This dance opens energy to understand relationships and activate love. They can awaken sexuality or release perceptions about problems in those areas. It can be used to link yourself with the fairy realms and to stimulate artistic inspiration. It manifests greater love and idealism. It can also be used to draw little things to us quickly, like quick cash.

SYMBOL: ♀   **FRAGRANCE:** Patchouli

COLOR: Green, pinks   **ROTATIONS:** Seven

MAGICKAL IMAGE: Beautiful, naked woman with a rose

MUSIC: Beethoven's Pastoral, Zamfir

Venus Dance Movements

A. In this movement, the arms coax new things to you with circling, drawing motions. The movements are slow and inviting. Sway as you coax.

Venus Dance Movements

B. In this movement, you are spread, open and ready, swaying and coaxing what you need and want to you. See yourself as magnetic energy, attracting life to you. Know that nothing can resist your charms. Use the conjuring gaze as described in chapter three.

Mars

This dance stimulates the energy of strength and power. It can be used to manifest opportunities to overcome cruelty or obstacles, to awaken courage and new perceptions, to reveal ways to tear down the old, and to manifest opportunities to do so. It is excellent to use anytime a major change is needed. It can also awaken critical judgment and can be used to obtain information on enemies and discord.

SYMBOL: ♂   **FRAGRANCE:** Cinnamon

COLOR: Red   **ROTATIONS:** Five

MAGICKAL IMAGE: Warrior with a sword

MUSIC: Wagner's Ride of the Valkyries, Pomp and Circumstance, marches

Mars Dance Movements

A. Raise up on your toes and tap your heels on the Earth in a cadence of five. As you tap your heels, raise your arms upward in the same rhythm, until they are high above your head. At the fifth count, circle your arms back to your chest. Repeat five times. Tapping and stomping raise energy.

B. Assume the Horse Stance. See yourself as strong and stable.

C. Move to the Shoulder Stand. This strengthens the shoulders, which are associated with Mars.

Mars Dance Movements

Jupiter

The dance movements for Jupiter open up expansiveness and abundance in our life. They can be used to awaken a greater sense of obedience to the higher powers or to provide opportunities for financial gain. It draws an energy of justice to us, stimulates prosperity and opportunities to manifest prosperity, and can also be used to hear the inner call of the quest. It is excellent for releasing an energy of peace, mercy, and higher understanding. It can also be used to overcome hypocrisy and bigotry that hinders us.

SYMBOL: ♃   FRAGRANCE: Bayberry

COLOR: Royal Blue   ROTATIONS: Four

MAGICKAL IMAGE: Throned king or queen holding a cornucopia

MUSIC: Franck's Panis Angelicus, Beethoven's Fifth Symphony

Jupiter Dance Movements

A. These movements, called *the Ropes of Abundance,* imitate the threads and ropes of life and how they are all tied together. The movements are circular, swinging the arms out and back around you, tying everything in the Universe to you. You are not separate from anything; you are tied to the abundance of it all. The swinging frees us to receive what we want. We are open to receive from the Universe.

B. This is the yoga posture, *The Fish*. It takes our legs away from us so we have to be open to receive from the Heavens. We draw our wealth from the Heavens, and as we learn that we are not truly separate from it, abundance opens on all levels.

C. This is a modified position of *The Fish*. Some find *The Fish* position uncomfortable, so this can serve in its place. When you dance Jupiter, be open to receive both little and big gifts. Failure to receive even compliments can stop the universal flow.

Jupiter Dance Movements (continued)

Saturn

Saturn is the great teacher, and these dance movements open us to the process of birth and death. This dance can be used to open understanding of past sorrows, burdens, and limitations. It can be used to stimulate new vision, clairvoyance, and opportunities for new birth. To dance Saturn is to be open to faithfulness, discipline, and the higher understanding of life. It is the dance of the womb from which comes life and learning, the source of primal creative energy. It can open the veils that hide the Akashic records.

SYMBOL: ♄   FRAGRANCE: Myrrh

COLOR: Black   ROTATIONS: Three

MAGICKAL IMAGE: Mature woman with cloak of concealment and life

MUSIC: Ave Maria, Brahm's Lullaby, Debussy's Clair de Lune

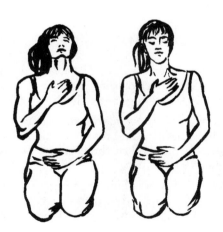

Saturn Dance Movements

A. With the left hand on womb and right hand on the heart, circle the head three times and then the trunk three times. The body leans forward with a soft movement, a symbol of coming out of the womb into new life and awareness. Repeat this three times.

Saturn Dance Movements (continued)

B. This movement for Saturn, called *The Old Tibetan Meditation Pose,* opens new insight and understanding. It makes everything brighter and more distinct. We can see things more clearly.

Begin by squatting, a position many societies used to give birth. Rest your elbows upon your knees, and place your thumbs in the inner corner of your eyes—the medial end of the eyebrow. It is stimulating to the third eye.

With the thumbs in this position, the fingers are brought together in prayer fashion over the forehead so that a triangle is formed around the third eye area. This triangle is also a symbol for the womb.

Steps to the Magickal Dance of the Planets

1. Familiarize yourself with the energies and correspondences of the planetary force you wish to dance into manifestation in your life.

2. Set the atmosphere with the appropriate fragrance, candles, colors, etc. You may even wish to paint the planetary symbol upon yourself as part of the ritual preparation and attunement.

3. Dance the sacred circle. Use the number of rotations listed for that particular planet. For example, if you are performing the dance for Venus, dance the sacred circle seven times.

4. As you dance the circle—two steps forward, one step back, visualize the circle filling with the color associated with the planet. Again, for example, if you are dancing Venus, see the sacred circle filling with vibrant green light and energy.

5. Also visualize the symbol for the planet inscribed inside the sacred circle.

6. Enter into the circle and perform the *Rending of the Veil*. As you do, see and feel the circle being flooded with even stronger energy associated with the planet. See the color grow more brilliant. Imagine the symbol for the planet glowing with crystalline white light.

7. Perform your balancing moves to stabilize yourself within this planetary force.

8. Begin to spin in place, using the number of rotations associated with the planet. As you do, see yourself taking on the appearance of the magickal image. See yourself becoming the embodiment of that planetary force. Eventually, you may wish to build the spinning up to the point where you repeat the rotation number three times.

9. Pause and allow yourself to become grounded into this image.

See and imagine everything you can do because of this ability to align with this great universal force.

Now back away from the center of the circle so that you can see the image of the planetary symbol on the floor before you. Then slowly walk the outline of that symbol. Know that with each step, you are forming an alliance with the planetary force it represent.

10. Having traced the symbol with your steps, move back to the center of the sacred circle. See yourself standing on that large symbol for the planet. Know that you are the master and director of all the forces associated with that planet and its power to influence and affect your life.

11. You can now move into the specific movements associated with the planet itself. As you do so, keep in mind the specific purpose for your activation of this planet's energy. See the magickal image come alive within you more strongly with each of the movements so that the purpose will be fulfilled.

12. Assume a meditative posture, and assimilate the energy. Visualize, imagine, and know that it is going to empower your life. See it working for you exactly the way you wish it to. See everything you will be able to accomplish because of this energy. Envision yourself receiving some confirmation within 24 hours that it has been set in motion for you.

13. Now stand and absorb into you the color, the symbol, and the magickal image. Feel them alive within you. Know that when you leave the circle you will take them to the outer world to work more effectively for you. When you have absorbed them all, perform the balancing movements again to stabilize them within your life.

14. Now take three steps back from the center and perform the *Closing of the Veils.*

15. Move to the perimeter of the sacred circle and perform the dance counter-clockwise to dissipate its energy until its ready to be opened again.

Magickal Dance: The Dance
of the Zodiac

A wonderful way to re-awaken the innate attunement to the stars is through dancing the actual constellations for the twelve zodiac signs.

Each sign of the zodiac has its own corresponding energies which affect us. We do not have to be born into a sign to feel its effects. Each time the sun moves into a new sign in the course of the year, the energies of that sign become more active in our lives.

Dancing the constellations is especially effective when performed at the time that the sun enters each sign. It strengthens our awareness of its influence within our lives and enables us to direct it more consciously. By the end of the year, you have danced the celestial energies into greater activity within your own life.

A powerful variation of this dance can be used around the time of your birthday. The time of your birthday is a powerful period in your life. It is known as the solar return. The inherent potentials that we came into life with are more active. Performing the dance for your astrological constellation helps you to stimulate these potentials even more strongly.

Three aspects of the astrological chart which strongly influence your physical life expression are your sun sign, moon sign, and the rising sign or ascendant. If you do not know what these are, inexpensive astrological charts that designate these can be found through most metaphysical bookstores. About seven days before your birthday, dance the constellations for each, culminating with the dance of your sun sign on the night before your birthday.

It is a good idea to occasionally dance the movements for your sun sign throughout the year. This keeps you in touch with your most basic energy patterns. Usually when we lose touch with our basic energy patterns, our lives become unbalanced. Dancing the constellation keeps us grounded and in a position to more easily evolve into higher expressions of our energy.

Steps for the Dance of the Zodiac

1. Begin by familiarizing yourself with basic information about your sun sign. Consult any basic astrology manual. Refer also to the charts on the following pages. Hold the image of the constellation firmly in your mind.

2. Set the atmosphere with appropriate incense, candles, etc. You may also wish to paint the constellation and its glyph on your hands or upon the part of the body associated with your sign. Refer to the chart on page 37.

3. Create the sacred space by dancing the circle at least three times. Visualize this as the stars revolve throughout the heavens. Also visualize the circle filling with the color or colors of the astrological sign.

4. Visualize the glyph or symbol for your astrological sign encompassing the inner circle within that color.

5. Enter into the circle and perform the *Rending of the Veils*. As you do, see and feel the color becoming stronger and more vibrant and the glyph beginning to glow.

6. Perform the balancing movements to stabilize yourself within this astrological force.

7. Perform the half wheel posture as depicted below. As you assume this position, feel the glyph being drawn into you.

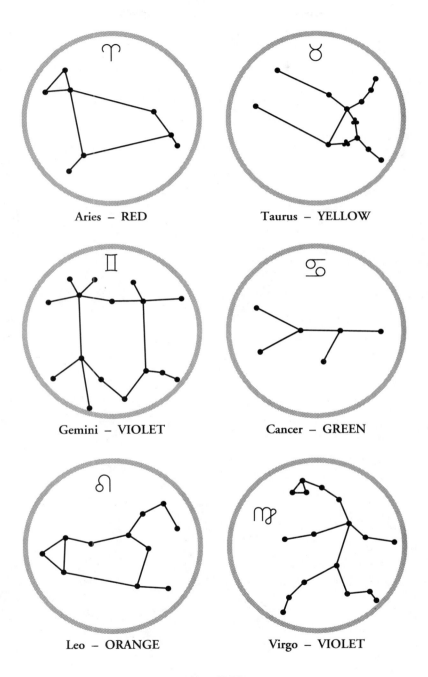

Aries – RED

Taurus – YELLOW

Gemini – VIOLET

Cancer – GREEN

Leo – ORANGE

Virgo – VIOLET

Constellations

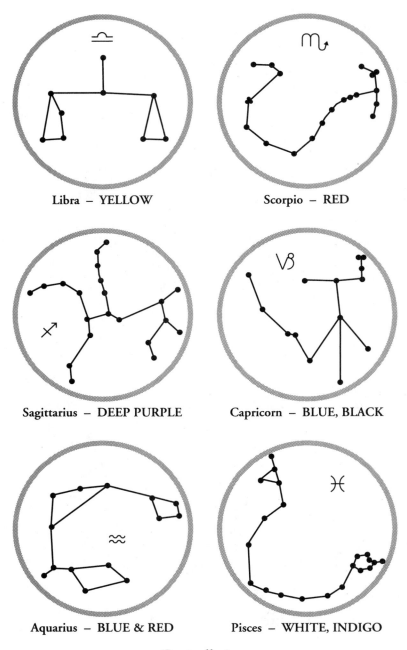

Libra – YELLOW

Scorpio – RED

Sagittarius – DEEP PURPLE

Capricorn – BLUE, BLACK

Aquarius – BLUE & RED

Pisces – WHITE, INDIGO

Constellations

Keep your head back as if your are looking into the heart of Heaven itself.

Imagine and know that by this movement you are re-imprinting the brain with the movements of the stars. You are setting the stars in motion around you. Hold this position, feeling yourself become a part of the heavens.

8. Open your eyes and raise up. As you do, see yourself within the midst of the stars of your constellation. Stand and step off the outline of the constellation as depicted on the next two pages.

9. A powerful way of activating the stars of the constellation is to spin at the points of the stars. Begin to step off the outline. As you come to a position where there is a star, spin three times in that place. See the star twinkling, shining with new life as you do.

10. After having danced the constellation, assume a meditative pose. Pull this outline into the area of the body it is associated with. Visualize it shining within you to fill you with its energy. See yourself as a microcosm where the heavenly forces play themselves out. Visualize all that you are capable of because of this stellar awakening.

11. Take three steps back and perform the *Closing of the Veils.*

12. Dance the sacred circle in reverse, knowing that the heavens have been brought to earth to fulfill you as you do.

CHAPTER ELEVEN

DANCING TO YOURSELF

Magickal dance is a means of celebrating life. It is a way of awakening innate power and energy. It is a way of celebrating the divine within ourselves. Magick is not something that is evil or negative. It is a way of understanding, healing, and honoring that which we have lost and forgotten.

We are all musical and we all have rhythm. It is intrinsic to our nature. We have been surrounded by music since the moment of conception, from the sounds carried to us through the amniotic fluids during pregnancy, to the rhythmic beat of our hearts. Rhythm is the pulse of life, and who has not seen a mother singing and humming softly while rocking a crying child? The sounds and the rocking restore a soothing rhythm to the child's metabolism.

We all can dance, whether we were trained or not. As children, we swayed and spun and lifted our feet in ways that were natural to us whenever we heard music. Observe young children at play. They often hum and sway to an inner song. Through magickal dance we reawaken that child. We celebrate that which is a part of us all and yet bigger than us all—the Dance of Life.

Magickal Dance: The Dance
of Birth and Death

Birth and death are natural. Humanity has always regarded both with great awe and fear. All of the ancient civilizations had ritualized procedures concerning them. Birth and death are the greatest changes we encounter, but they are not the only ones. We experience birth and death on many levels every day.

Any change can be seen as a birth and a death. Changes are blessings. They signal new growth. They signaled the tearing down of the old and building up of the new. We are each challenged in our lives to release the old and embrace the new.

If we are to take advantage of the opportunities that such an experiences in the physical can create, we must understand the rites of passage. A rite of passage is a celebration of a transition within one's life. The Jewish Bar Mitzvah is a rite of passage from boyhood into manhood. We can use magickal dance to facilitate and initiate transitions within our own life circumstances:

1. Begin by deciding what you wish to change or what transition has come upon you.

2. Create your sacred space and *Open the Veils*. To enhance the effects, you may wish to visualize the inner circle filling with alternating circles of black and white. With practice you will have no difficulty holding this image in mind.

3. Balance yourself.

4. Then, slowly and very deliberately, perform each of the movements on the following pages. The first movement is the corpse pose shown in figure A. It symbolizes the death of the old. From death comes new birth, figure B. After birth, we begin to lift ourself into new expressions of energy, figure C. Pause and see yourself stabilizing within the new, upon a solid foundation. Now stand and perform the *Tibetan Walk to Nowhere*. Visualize and imagine yourself rising to new heights of achievement. You have joined the old with the new into new fulfillment.

5.   As you go through the movements, see yourself moving through the change you desire or the change that is occurring. See and feel all that you hope to experience. Imagine and know that as you rise to new life, all is born anew in greater love, abundance, prosperity, and fulfillment. Speak an affirmation of such.

6.   Take three steps back and close the veils, knowing the change will be smooth and beneficial.

7.   Dissipate the sacred space and allow the energies of transition to work for you. Know your rite of passage will bless your life.

A.   When we go through transitions, we die to the old to be born to the new. Assume the corpse pose in figure A, see the old you and the old situation dying off. We then are born into the new.

B. Roll to your side and take a fetal position. See yourself being born.

C. Then rise from the fetal to the sitting position, symbolic of a new foundation solid within the new energy.

Dance of Birth and Death (continued)

D. Then rise to a standing position and begin the *Tibetan Walk to Nowhere*. This is a walk to new fulfillment, abundance, prosperity, and joy.

As you dance the *Tibetan Walk to Nowhere*, see yourself being fulfilled in as many ways as possible with this transition. Visualize it all occurring with ease. Then assume the last position, figure D, at a new position of great fulfillment. You have your feet firmly upon a new foundation with your arms and hands extended to take in the fruits and rewards of this change.

Dance of Birth and Death (continued)

Magickal Dance: Spinning Our Hidden Energies Into Life

One of the great mystical secrets of humanity lies hidden within our names. The meaning, the sounds, the rhythms, the nature of the letters, and all of their combinations can reveal secrets about our past, present and future essence. Our individual names contain much power and much significance. If we come to understand and apply these significances, we can discover much about our individual purpose and release our spiritual energies more dynamically into the physical world.

Our first name is an energy signature. It reflects our most creative essence. The vowels are our most significant aspect. The vowels indicate the life force we have come to awaken most fully. They are representative of the unseen spiritual force within. The consonants reflect the energies that we have brought with us from our past lives to help us unfold that inner potential represented by the vowels. We can use magickal dance to bring these energies alive.

1. Begin by reviewing the charts on the next three pages. They provide some of the correspondences associated with the letters of the alphabet. On a piece of paper or within a notebook, write out your full first name at birth. Then write down the associations for each letter. This will help you remember them. For more information on their significance, refer to my other books, *Sacred Power in Your Name* and *The Magickal Name.*

2. Then using the chart below determine the number associated with each letter of your name:

1	2	3	4	5	6	7	8	9
A	B	C	D	E	F	G	H	I
J	K	L	M	N	O	P	Q	R
S	T	U	V	W	X	Y	Z	

For each letter in your name, you should now have a keynote, a color, and a number. The number determines the rotations of the spin.

For example:

> M = regrowth and rebirth; mother of pearl; 4
> A = illumination; white; 1
> R = love, wisdom, and freedom; orange; 9
> Y = transmutation; golden brown; 7

3. Keeping these in mind, create your sacred space by dancing the circle. Take three steps in and *Open the Veils*. Perform your balancing movements to stabilize the energy.

4. Focus upon your name and its significance. Begin with the first letter and spin in place the number of rotations as determined above. As you do, see the color of the letter swirling about you. At the end of the spinning, pause and reflect upon the keynote and meaning of this letter. Think about how you can apply it to your life. Then absorb the color energy into yourself. Repeat this with each letter of your name.

5. After spinning each letter and absorbing its corresponding energy, assume a posture for the primary vowel within your first name. This is the vowel most strongly accented and pronounced in your name. See yourself in your most powerful magickal image. Meditate upon the entire significance and power of all the letters. Visualize and feel their energies alive within you. Visualize how you will be able to apply those energies in all areas of your life.

6. After this, give a prayer or affirmation of thanks and take three steps back from the center and *Close the Veils*.

7. Leave the inner circle and perform the dance to dissipate the sacred space until next called upon. Know that you are empowered as you do this.

A = Ethers
Keynote = Illumination
Colors = White or Light Blue

I = Fire
Keynote = Divine Love
Colors = Red Violet or Opal

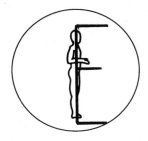

E = Air
Keynote = Strength/Self-mastery
Colors = Blue or Dark Violet

O = Water
Keynote = Justice/Balance
Colors = Black or Dark Ultra-
            marine

U = Earth
Keynote = Birth Giving
Colors = Earth tones and
            Ivory Black

Y = Fire
Keynote = Transmutation
Colors = Lt. Golden Brown and
            Pink

Power and Postures of Vowels

LETTER	KEYNOTE OF LETTER	COLOR	ASTROLOGY
A	Higher wisdom and illumination	White/Lt.Blue	Ether/Uranus
B	Creative power of wisdom	Yellow	Mercury
C	Creative cyclic expression	Red-Orange	Moon
D	Fertility	Emerald	Venus
E	Perception and universality	Blue	Air/Mercury
F	Fulfillment through harmony	Lt. Red-Orange	Taurus
G	Faith and discernment	Deep Blue	Moon
H	Power of the word, imagination, and intuition	Bright Reds	Aries
I	Divine love	Red Violet	Fire/Mars
J	Harvesting cosmic love	Yellow Green	Virgo
K	New journeys through creativity	Blue Violet	Jupiter
L	Magnetism and power of attraction	Emerald	Libra
M	Regrowth and rebirth	Mother of Pearl	Neptune/Moon
N	Willed transmutation	Blue-Green	Scorpio
O	Justice and balance	Black	Water/Saturn
P	Power of hidden expression	Scarlet	Mars
Q	Intelligence of the heart	Violet	Pisces

LETTER	KEYNOTE OF LETTER	COLOR	ASTROLOGY
R	Fires of love, wisdom, and freedom	Orange-Amber	Sun
S	The serpent wisdom	Blue	Sagittarius
T	Inspiration for spiritual warriorship	Green-Yellow/ Amber	Leo
U	Birth giving	Earth tones	Earth/Venus
V	Fruitfulness and openness	Red-orange	Taurus
W	Uniting of consciousness	Green/Silver	Venus/Moon
X	Force of duality	Deep indigo	Sagittarius/ Jupiter
Y	Transmutation and alchemy	Lt. golden brown	Fire and water/ Venus and Mars
Z	Lightning force	Pastel orange	Gemini
CH	Higher vision	Amber	Cancer
PH	Ancient well of knowledge	Orange-brown	Pluto
SH	Awakening the inner fires	Orange-scarlet	Fire/Uranus
TH	Opening of the gateway	Deep indigo	Saturn
TZ	Creative imagination	Violet	Aquarius

Magickal Dance: Dancing the Sacred Name Talisman

Most of the ancient alphabets were considered sacred. They were tools to teach the mysteries of the universe. Most had a variety of correspondences and reflected specific kinds of energy plays, based upon the color associated with the letters, the number associated with the letters, the astrological correspondence, and the shapes of the letters themselves.

One of the ways of personalizing talismans and amulets is by converting your name to one of the ancient alphabets. Simply writing our name in an ancient script forces us to pay attention and concentrate on the energies associated with it.

We can visualize the dance circle as the sacred talisman. We can then dance and step out our name in the ancient script form. This activates the ancient magick of that script and brings it into manifestation through the sacred circle. These can also be used to decorate our robes and our body.

We can paint our name in that script upon the body, again as a way of more intensely invoking the archetypal energies represented by it and working through us because of our alignment with the name.

You are presented with eight magickal alphabets—the Egyptian, Phoenician, Hebrew, Greek, Theban, Runic, Ogham, and the Malachim. The Egyptian is primarily a pictograph and thus is not as easy to dance to, although it can be used to decorate body and ritual attire. The Phoenician was the basis of many alphabets and their esoteric teachings. The Hebrew alphabet was considered the 22 steps to wisdom. Greece was a place of great magic and thus its alphabet maintains that energy connection. The Theban alphabet was designed for the Old Religion, Wicca and forms of paganism. Dancing it is flowing and artistic. The runic alphabet has specific postures associated with it, called stodhur.[2] The Ogham was a tree alphabet of the ancient Druids and Celts. The Malachim was an alphabet originally designed for high forms of ritual magic.

[2] Edred Thorrson, *Futhark—A Handbook of Rune Magick.* (Samuel Weiser; York Beach, 1984).

1. Begin by drawing a talismanic form, as depicted below. Then using one of the ancient alphabets given, write your name within the dance talisman area. Keep in mind some of the significances of your name as we learned in the previous section. Choose an alphabet you are drawn to. If you have an interest in a particular tradition or mythology for which there is an alphabet, use it.

2. Space the letters of your name around the inside perimeter of the circle. When you get ready to dance this talisman, it will be important to connect each letter with movement. You can use the *Tibetan Walk to Nowhere*, or you can improvise movements. In our example, we will use a flowing, spinning motion to connect one letter with the next.

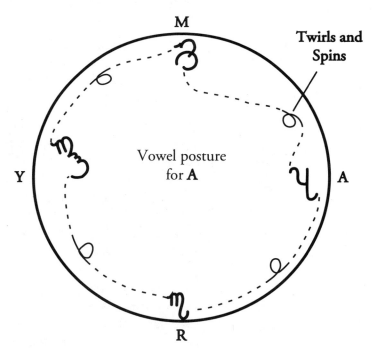

3. Convert your name to an ancient alphabet and arrange the letters around the inside perimeter of the circle as we did with the name MARY, using the Theban alphabet.

4. Now visualize yourself stepping off each letter in turn, and dancing from one to the next so there is a constant flow. Complete the circle by dancing from the last letter back to the first.

5. Step back into the center of the circle. See and feel the Talisman vibrating with energy. Assume the posture associated with your primary vowel, meditate upon and absorb this energy into every aspect of your being.

6. You may wish to write your name several times in this script to familiarize yourself with it. Practice stepping off the formation as it is depicted upon your talisman design.

7. Set the atmosphere for your dance ritual. Create the sacred space and enter the circle. Open the veils and balance the energy with the appropriate movements. You may wish to speak a prayer or affirmation of what you hope to achieve by awakening the ancient and archetypal energies associated with your name.

   This particular exercise is strengthening, protective, and harmonizing to the entire energy field. It can be used whenever we are feeling out of touch or unbalanced.

8. You may wish to spin yourself into your magickal image, as we learned to do earlier in this work. Then move to the space within the inner circle where you will dance the first letter of your name. Step off the formation of the first letter. Be creative and conscious of the energy you are invoking with this movement.

9.   Then free-dance to the position of the second letter in your name and step off its outline. As you step the letters off, you can strengthen the effect by visualizing them being inscribed in that position in brilliant crystalline light. Do this in turn with each letter, until you return to your starting point at the first letter.

10.   Now step back to the center of the circle. See and feel your name alive within this circle, acting as a life-size talisman of power and health.

11.   Assume the posture associated with the primary vowel within your name, and meditate upon the energies that have been brought to life. Visualize how you will apply them and keep them strong .

12.   Stand, if your are not already doing so, and draw each letter back into yourself. Feel yourself empowered as they each become a part of you and your life hereafter. See yourself in your magickal image.

13.   Balance these energies with the appropriate movements. Take three steps back and *Close the Veils*. Now dissipate the circle and take out into your daily life greater power and light.

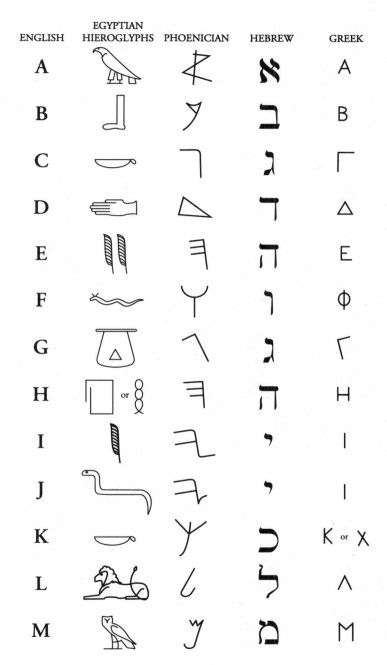

Talismanic Alphabets

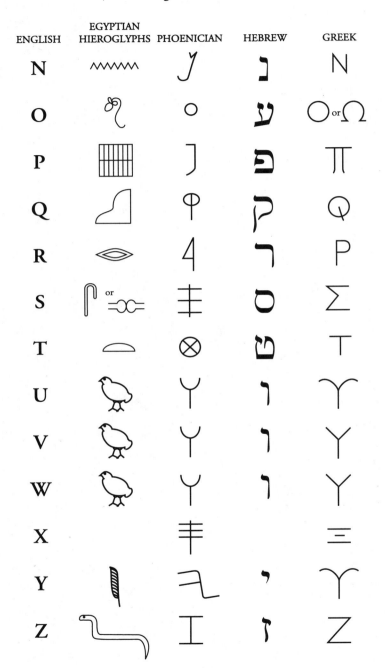

Talismanic Alphabets

ENGLISH	THEBAN	RUNIC	OGHAM	MALACHIM
A				
B				
C				
D				
E				
F				
G				
H				
I				
J		or		
K				
L				
M				

Talismanic Alphabets

ENGLISH	THEBAN	RUNIC	OGHAM	MALACHIM
N				
O				
P				
Q				
R				
S				
T				
U				
V				
W				
X				
Y				
Z				

Talismanic Alphabets

Magickal Dance: Color Dancing for Health

One of the most effective means of dancing for health is through the use of color. Chromotherapy is growing in its popularity as a holistic healing technique. We can use color in dance to assist us in our own health. It is simply a matter of creating a sacred space where we can more easily absorb the colors.

1. Begin by determining which color or colors you may need. The table on the following page will help you.

2. Set the atmosphere. Light candles within the dance area of the color you intend to invoke and use.

3. You may wish to wear clothing or a robe of the appropriate color.

4. Create your sacred circle. Perform seven revolutions, symbolic of the rainbow spectrum. As you do, see the inner circle filling with the color or colors you need or desire.

5. Step into the circle and open the veils. Feel and see these colors intensifying and strengthening. See the color as a living force.

6. Perform your balancing exercises.

7. Assume a meditation posture, and breathe in the color within the circle. As you slowly inhale and exhale, see and feel this color heal and strengthen you. If there is a particular area you are working on healing, see this occur. Know that the dance opened this area to receive the healing color more effectively. The dance breaks down mental barriers to the healing process.

8. You may also wish to perform the *Sun and Moon Breath Dance* described in chapter two. With the breaths and the movements, simply assimilate the color.

9. Take time to feel yourself healed and strengthened. If performed before bedtime, affirm that during the night, the colors will continue to work for you—to heal you by morning.

10. Take three steps back from the center and close the veils. Dissipate the circle knowing you have given yourself one of the most effective healing treatments possible.

TABLE OF COLORS

White .... Strengthening, purifying, stimulates creativity, use to amplify the effects of other colors

Black .... Protective, grounding, calming—use sparingly and with other colors

Red .... Stimulating, warms, good for colds and circulation, awakens passion and sex, good for the blood

Orange .... Awakens joy and wisdom, socialness, emotions, good for muscular system, re-vitalizing

Yellow .... Affects mental faculties, stimulates enthusiasm, digestive system, adrenal glands, optimism

Green .... Balancing, increases sensitivity, soothing to nerves, restful

Green-blues .... Extremely healing; this color should never be used with cancerous or tumorous conditions because it stimulates growth

Blue .... Cooling and relaxing; quiets; antiseptic; strengthens respiratory system; good for high blood pressure and all childhood diseases; awakens intuition and creativity

Indigo .... Very healing on all levels; awakens intuition; blood purifier; balances hemispheres of brain; good for obsessions

Violet .... Affects skeletal system; antiseptic; cleansing and detoxifying; stimulates inspiration and humility; awakens dream activity

APPENDIX OF DANCE RITUALS

There are many dance rituals that can be employed by anyone wishing to do some exploration and experimentation. The following is by no means a complete list, but it simply provides a starting point for anyone wishing to go further. The means of choreographing them is left, for the most part, up to the individual. Remember that dance is creative and it is natural. If you can move, you can dance!

Dances of Blessings and Introductions

These can be blessings and dances for a new child, a new job, etc. The dance should invoke, ease, and bless. Assumptions of god-forms can be easily adapted for this. It helps introduce the new energy and blessing more harmoniously.

Fertility Dances

Dances of fertility have been common in most areas of the world. There have been male fertility dances and female fertility dances. The purpose and function of such can vary from honoring and celebrating one's own sexuality and coming of age, to stimulating sexual arousal and raising spiritual sight through sexual union.

Fertility dances stimulate harmony and unity in groups and in couples. They are powerfully effective when combined with tantric techniques of sexual union to raise the kundalini and lift the spiritual awareness of the couple.

A good way to begin such development of unity in groups and couples is through movement that involves contact improvisation. In this exercise, one person will lead and the other will follow. Begin by having the two individuals touch wrist to wrist. The key is to maintain physical contact throughout the dance. The contact at the wrists can be given up as long as physical contact is maintained somewhere between the two individuals.

Movement should be slow, easy, and free, so the individuals can follow each other. Bending, raising, turning, or sliding—any movement is acceptable as long as both individuals can maintain some physical contact. This kind of practice cultivates sensuousness and even sexuality. It also develops harmony between the two. An interesting phenomena of such exercises is that while one individual may initially lead, after several minutes, both are attuning to and anticipating the next movements and continual contact is more easily facilitated.

A variation from this is what has been called mirror dancing. This is especially effective for creating harmony and raising sensual and sexual energy in the participants. One participant faces the other and will serve as a mirror. Any move that is made should be mirrored by this individual. The participants can move close to each other, but actual physical contact should be avoided—at least in the initial phases of a mirror dance ritual. Mirroring in psychology is a means of establishing rapport and breaking down barriers. It develops resonance and rapport between the two dancers.

In magickal dance, this is especially powerful with someone who is a tantric partner or with whom one is building a deeper relationship. This can also be used within the sacred space of magickal dance when the dancers become the priest and priestess of the ritual. The union of the gods and goddesses can be initiated through such movement to release powerful psychic currents.

Healing Dances

Healing dances can be as simple as those described in the last chapter which use color to heal, or they can become as intricately therapeutic as recreating a past trauma through dance and moving into a healing outcome that does not have remaining repercussions. Experimentation is being performed on assisting adult victims of child abuse in releasing all trauma of the abuse and all cellular imprints through dance. It is best that such intense healing dances be supervised by a qualified individual.

Celebrations of Nature

These dances can be as simple as dancing around a tree to awaken its energy and blessing, to dancing the changes of the seasons and the cycles of the moon. Each change of season and cycle of the moon has its own corresponding energy pattern. These patterns affect us whether we realize it or not. One way of increasing awareness of the effects is through dance ritual to intensify their play within our lives. A study of basic astrology can reflect lunar and astrological changes.

The seasonal changes also bring their own corresponding energies which can be attuned to and invoked more dynamically through dance:

Autumn Equinox

Time of harvest, seed planting, and recapitulation. It is the time of cleaning out the old and sowing seeds for the new.

Winter Solstice

Activates the feminine energies. It is a time to attune to the angelic kingdom and to go within oneself to awaken intuition, illumination, and creative imagination.

Vernal Equinox

Activates the masculine energies. It is a time to assert and express yourself, to begin greater work on the seeds you have been sowing since the fall season.

Summer Solstice

A time to celebrate nature and to balance the male and female energies. It is a time of fertility and birth.

Storytelling Dances

Many myths and tales are aligned with archetypal energies. Dancing them in ritual space will manifest similar energies and experiences in your life. You can then utilize these energies.

BIBLIOGRAPHY

Costumes of the Ancient World (Series). New York: Chelsea House Publications, 1987.

Adams, Doug and Apostolos-Cappodona, Diane. *Dance as Religious Study.* New York: Crossroads Press, 1990.

Alkema, Chester Jay. *Monster Masks.* New York: Sterling Publications, 1973.

Ashcroft-Nowicki, Dolores. *First Steps in Ritual.* Northamptonshire: Aquarian Press, 1982.

_____. *Ritual Magic Workbook.* Northamptonshire: Aquarian Press, 1986.

Beck, Lilla and Wilson, Annie. *What Colour Are You?* Great Britain: Turnstone Press, 1981.

Bellamak, Lu. *Dancing Prayers.* Arizona: Cybury Graphics, 1982.

Brain, Robert. *The Decorated Body.* New York: Harper and Row, 1979.

Buckland, Raymond. *The Complete Book of Witchcraft.* St. Paul: Llewellyn Publications, 1988.

Cohen, Robert. *The Dance Workshop.* New York: Simon and Schuster, 1986.

Copeland, Roger and Cohen, Marsha. *What Is Dance?* New York: Oxford University Press, 1983.

Davies, Sir John. "Penelope Full of Dance," *Orchestra,* 1596.

Douglas, Nik and Slinger, Penny. *Sexual Secrets.* New York: Destiny Books, 1979.

Fonteyn, Margot. *The Magic of Dance.* New York: Alfred A. Knopf, 1979.

Grater, Michael. *Complete Book of Mask Making.* New York: Dover Publications, 1967.

Haberland, Wolfgang. *The Art of North America.* New York: Crown Publishers, 1964.

Highwater, Jamake. *Dance—Ritual of Experience.* New York: Alfred Van Der Marck Editions, 1978.

Hittleman, Richard. *Guide for the Seeker*. New York: Bantam Books, 1978.

_____. *Introduction to Yoga*. New York: Bantam Books, 1975.

Humphrey, Doris. *The Art of Making Dances*. New York: Grove Press Inc., 1980.

Joyce, Mary. *Dance Techniques for Children*. California: Mayfield Publication Company, 1984.

Kalinin, Beverly. *Power to the Dancers!* Portland: Metamorphous Press, 1988.

Kraus, Richard. *History of Dance*. Englewood Cliffs: Prentice-Hall, Inc., 1969.

Laws, Kenneth. *The Physics of Dance*. New York: Schirmer Books, 1984.

Lawson, Joan. *Teaching Young Dancers*. New York: Theatre Arts Books, 1975.

Mattlage, Louise. *Dances of Faith*. Pennsylvania: County Press.

Novack, Cynthia J. *Sharing the Dance*. Madison: University of Wisconsin Press, 1990.

Peters, Joan and Sutcliffe, Anna. Boston: *Creative Masks for Stage and School*. Plays Inc., 1975.

Seitering, Carolyn. *The Liturgy As Dance*. New York: Crossroads Publishing, 1984.

Sherbon, Elizabeth. *On the Count of One*. Chicago: Chicago Review Press, 1990.

Snook, Barbara. *Making Masks for School Plays*. Boston: Plays Inc., 1972.

Sorell, Walter. *Dance Has Many Faces*. New York: Columbia University Press, 1966.

Tegner, Bruce. *Kung Fu and Tai Chi*. California: Thor Publishing, 1973.

Thevoz, Michel. *The Painted Body*. New York: Rizzoli Publishing, 1984.

Wilson, Chaz. *Martial Dance*. Northamptonshire: Aquarian Press, 1988.

Zarina, Xenia. *Classic Dances of the Orient*. New York: Crown Publishing, 1967.

STAY IN TOUCH

On the following pages you will find listed, with their current prices, some of the books now available on related subjects. Your book dealer stocks most of these and will stock new titles in the Llewellyn series as they become available. We urge your patronage.

To obtain our full catalog, to keep informed about new titles as they are released and to benefit from informative articles and helpful news, you are invited to write for our bimonthly news magazine/catalog, Llewellyn's *New Worlds of Mind and Spirit*. A sample copy is free, and it will continue coming to you at no cost as long as you are an active mail customer. Or you may subscribe for just $7.00 in the U.S.A. and Canada ($20.00 overseas, first class mail). Many bookstores also have New Worlds available to their customers. Ask for it.

Stay in touch! In New Worlds' pages you will find news and features about new books, tapes and services, announcements of meetings and seminars, articles helpful to our readers, news of authors, products and services, special money-making opportunities, and much more.

Llewellyn's New Worlds of Mind and Spirit
P.O. Box 64383-004, St. Paul, MN 55164-0383, U.S.A.

* * *

TO ORDER BOOKS AND TAPES

If your book dealer does not have the books described on the following pages readily available, you may order them directly from the publisher by sending full price in U.S. funds, plus $3.00 for postage and handling for orders under $10.00; $4.00 for orders over $10.00. There are no postage and handling charges for orders over $50.00. Postage and handling rates are subject to change. UPS Delivery: We ship UPS whenever possible. Delivery guaranteed. Provide your street address as UPS does not deliver to P.O. Boxes. UPS to Canada requires a $50.00 minimum order. Allow 4-6 weeks for delivery. Orders outside the U.S.A. and Canada: Airmail—add retail price of book; add $5.00 for each non-book item (tapes, etc.); add $1.00 per item for surface mail.

FOR GROUP STUDY AND PURCHASE

Because there is a great deal of interest in group discussion and study of the subject matter of this book, we feel that we should encourage the adoption and use of this particular book by such groups by offering a special quantity price to group leaders or agents.

Our Special Quantity Price for a minimum order of five copies of *Magickal Dance* is $29.85 cash-with-order. This price includes postage and handling within the United States. Minnesota residents must add 6.5% sales tax. For additional quantities, please order in multiples of five. For Canadian and foreign orders, add postage and handling charges as above. Credit card (VISA, MasterCard, American Express) orders are accepted. Charge card orders only ($15.00 minimum order) may be phoned in free within the U.S.A. or Canada by dialing 1-800-THE-MOON. For customer service, call 1-612-291-1970. Mail orders to:

LLEWELLYN PUBLICATIONS
P.O. Box 64383-004, St. Paul, MN 55164-0383, U.S.A.

HOW TO HEAL WITH COLOR
by Ted Andrews
Now, for perhaps the first time, color therapy is placed within the grasp of the average individual. Anyone can learn to facilitate and accelerate the healing process on all levels with the simple color therapies in *How to Heal with Color*. Color serves as a vibrational remedy that interacts with the human energy system to stabilize physical, emotional, mental, and spiritual conditions. When there is balance, we can more effectively rid ourselves of toxins, negativities, and patterns that hinder our life processes.

0-87542-005-2, 240 pgs., mass market, illus. $3.95

HOW TO UNCOVER YOUR PAST LIVES
by Ted Andrews
Knowledge of your past lives can be extremely rewarding. It can assist you in opening to new depths within your own psychological makeup and provide greater insight into present circumstances with loved ones, career and health.

Now Ted Andrews shares with you nine different techniques that you can use to access your past lives. Between techniques, Andrews discusses issues such as karma and how it is expressed in your present life; the source of past life information; soul mates and twin souls; proving past lives; the mysteries of birth and death; animals and reincarnation; abortion and pre-mature death; and the role of reincarnation in Christianity.

0-87542-022-2, 240 pgs., mass market, illus. $3.95

HOW TO SEE AND READ THE AURA
by Ted Andrews
Everyone has an aura—the three-dimensional, shape-and-color-changing energy field that surrounds all matter. And anyone can learn to see and experience the aura more effectively. There is nothing magical about the process. It simply involves a little understanding, time, practice and perseverance.

Do some people make you feel drained? Do you find some rooms more comfortable and enjoyable to be in? Have you ever been able to sense the presence of other people before you actually heard or saw them? If so, you have experienced another person's aura. In this practical, easy-to-read manual, you receive a variety of exercises to practice alone and with partners to build your skills in aura reading and interpretation. Also, you will learn to balance your aura each day to keep it vibrant and strong so others cannot drain your vital force.

0-87542-013-3, 160 pgs., mass market, illus. $3.95

HOW TO MEET & WORK WITH SPIRIT GUIDES
by Ted Andrews
We often experience spirit contact in our lives but fail to recognize it for what it is. Now you can learn to access and attune to beings such as guardian angels, nature spirits and elementals, spirit totems, archangels, gods and goddesses—as well as family and friends after their physical death. Through a series of simple exercises, you can safely and gradually increase your awareness of spirits and your ability to identify them.

0-87542-008-7, 192 pgs., mass market, illus. $3.95

SACRED SOUNDS
Transformation through Music & Word
by Ted Andrews

Sound has always been considered a direct link between humanity and the divine. The ancient mystery schools all taught their students the use of sound as a creative and healing force that bridged the different worlds of life and consciousness.

Now, *Sacred Sounds* reveals to today's seekers how to tap into the magical and healing aspects of voice, resonance and music. On a physical level, these techniques have been used to alleviate aches and pains, lower blood pressure and balance hyperactivity in children. On a metaphysical level, they have been used to induce altered states of consciousness, open new levels of awareness, stimulate intuition and increase creativity.

In this book, Ted Andrews reveals the tones and instruments that affect the chakras, the use of kinesiology and "muscle testing" in relation to sound responses, the healing aspects of vocal tones, the uses of mystical words of power, the art of magical storytelling, how to write magical sonnets, how to form healing groups and utilize group toning for healing and enlightenment, and much, much more.

0-87542-018-4, 240 pgs., 5 1/4 x 8, illus., softcover $7.95

DREAM ALCHEMY
Shaping Our Dreams to Transform Our Lives
by Ted Andrews

What humanity is rediscovering is that what we dream can become real. Learning to shift the dream to reality and the reality to dream—to walk the thread of life between the worlds—to become a shapeshifter, a dreamwalker, is available to all. We have the potential to stimulate dream awareness for greater insight and fulfillment, higher inspiration and ultimately even controlled out-of-body experiences. It is all part of the alchemical process of the soul.

Through the use of our ancient myths and tales, we can initiate a process of dream alchemy. Through control of the dream state and its energies, we are put in touch with realities and energies that can open us to greater productivity during our waking hours. Learn to alter sleep conditions and increase dream activity through the use of herbs, fragrances, crystals, flower essences, totems, talismans and mandalas.

For those just opening to the psychic and spiritual realms, this is one of the safest and easiest ways to bridge your consciousness to higher realms.

0-897542-017-6, 264 pgs., 6 x 9, illus., softcover $12.95

16 STEPS TO HEALTH AND ENERGY
A Program of Color & Visual Meditation, Movement & Chakra Balance
by Pauline Wills & Theo. Gimble

Before an illness reaches your physical body, it has already been in your auric body for days, weeks, even months. By the time you feel sick, something in your life has been out of balance for a while. But why wait to get sick to get healthy? Follow the step-by-step techniques in *16 Steps to Health and Energy*, and you will open up the energy circuits of your subtle body so you are better able to stay balanced and vital in our highly toxic and stressful world.

Our subtle anatomy includes the "energy" body of 7 chakras that radiate the seven colors of the spectrum. Each chakra responds well to a particular combination of yoga postures and color visualizations, all of which are provided in this book.

At the end of the book is a series of 16 "workshops" that help you to travel through progressive stages of consciousness expansion and self-transformation. Each session deals with a particular color and all of its associated meditations, visualizations and yoga postures. Here is a truly holistic route to health at all levels! Includes 16 color plates!

0-87542-871-1, 224 pgs., 6 x 9, illus., softcover   **$12.95**

IMAGICK
Qabalistic Pathworking for Imaginative Magicians
by Ted Andrews

The Qabala, or "Tree of Life," is a productive and safe system of evolvement—one of the most effective means for tapping the energies of the universe. But it is not enough to study the Qabala; intellectual studies of the correspondences will not generate any magickal changes nor will a mere arousal of the energies. In order to achieve your hopes, dreams and wishes, you must also bring the Qabala into your day-to-day life. You must practice *Imagick*.

Imagick is a process of using the Qabala with visualization, meditation and imaging—in conjunction with physical movement—to stimulate electrical responses in the brain that help bridge your normal consciousness with your spiritual consciousness. The Imagick techniques, and especially the pathworking techniques described throughout this book, are powerfully effective. Their repeated use will build roadways between the outer and inner worlds, creating a flow that augments your energies, abilities and potentials.

There is a great mystique associated with the occult practice of pathworking. Pathworking shows you your blockages and brings them out so that you must deal with them. You open up the channels that create transition—a cleaning out of the debris you have accumulated. The pathworking techniques in this book make you face what you have not faced, search out hidden fears, overcome them and open yourself to yet higher and stronger knowledge and experience. Dance the Tree of Life and open the inner temples of your soul with *Imagick*.

0-87542-016-8, 312 pgs., 6 x 9, softcover   **$12.95**